The Fading Pips Trick

Place the three of hearts on the bottom of the deck with the ace of hearts immediately above it. Cover each of the two end pips of this bottom card with a thumb, so that only the middle pip is visible. Announce that the ace of hearts is on the bottom. The spectators will see the indices or realize from the awkward position of your hands that you are trying to pass the three as the ace. Turn the pack over, performing the glide and laying the real ace of hearts on the table.

Pretend to overhear one of the audience make an uncomplimentary remark regarding your skill as a prestidigitator. Of course, you may not have to pretend. Look hurt. Ask this spectator to turn over the card.

—from Chapter 8, "Sudden Stuff"

BILL TURNER

HOW TO

WITH

DO TRICKS
CARDS

Foreword by Henry Hay

Illustrated by Nelson Hahne

COLLIER BOOKS
NEW YORK, N.Y.

This Collier Books edition is published by arrangement with David McKay Company, Inc.

Collier Books is a division of The Crowell-Collier Publishing Company

First Collier Books Edition 1963

Foreword

WHEN THE PUBLISHERS ASKED me for professional advice about publishing Bill Turner's *The Card Wizard,** I could only say, "This is the book I was going to write next." Neither he nor I had ever seen a line of each other's stuff before; yet you might think all our books came from the same typewriter.

As my father used to observe when rereading his own work. "Naturally one likes to read good writing on subjects one cares about." And make no mistake, this is good writing about card tricks. The beginner has not been offered such a sound, lively, or instructive book on card magic in several decades. And the old hand can still learn things from these pages. I know I did.

Good card tricks brightly done are an inexhaustible entertainment, whereas any card trick ill done renders its performer a social pest. If you have chosen Bill Turner to guide you, you have done right by your long-suffering friends: you will become an entertainer, not a parlor menace.

The fact that Turner makes the art easy instead of hard is just a bonus you get for buying his merchandise.

Everyone concerned is grateful to Nelson Hahne for his expertly illuminating pictures.

HENRY HAY

* The original title of the book.—Ed.

Preface

THERE IS EVIDENCE that playing cards were in use in Egypt in the time of Joseph. Since that time there must have lived thousands of screwballs who sat up nights thinking up card tricks. No doubt, many of these characters—like the ingenious Joe Berg, who seldom puts down his deck except to wait on a customer in his Chicago magic shop—have been more than married to the pasteboards.

So it would be sheer conceit on my part to presume that the trick based on scarring the edge of the pack, for instance, had never been worked out by anyone else. Even if it should never have been exactly duplicated, it is still a variation of the old pencil-marked-edge ruse—which is a variation of the one-way principle. And all these devices are applications of the general principle of marking the cards—which can be only the merest trifle younger than the gaming pieces themselves.

All card tricks are based on principles that were originated long ago. Robert-Houdin, the magician sent by the French government to Algeria to awe the Arabs in 1852, wrote descriptions of the second-deal, the pass, the palm, pre-arranged cards, and the four-ace trick. The glide was known in the time of George Washington. And Scot's *Discoverie of Witchcraft,* which was a handbook for Shakespeare, discloses the principle of the gambler's shuffle! There is no telling how old these bits of trickery were before they broke into print.

Through the years, card tricksters have modified and reapplied these old principles, and they are still doing it.

So most good card tricks are evolved, not invented. Occasionally, an individual modifies a basic artifice in a way original enough to earn him the moral right to having his name associated with the resultant trick. No line can be drawn, of course, to determine when a trick is "original enough"; and controversy about this subject is endless. Sadly—in an otherwise wholesome art—piracy and plagiarism are common. In the scramble with which a new trick is received, a deserving originator is often forgotten. As a result of all this confusion, it is frequently impossible to trace even a recent trick through the maze of conflicting claims on each of its variations, and to determine its true source.

To the best of my knowledge, every trick described in this volume is a refinement of contributions made by many brains. If I have failed to give credit where it is due, the omission has been made by the conjuring fraternity in general and is not the result of a lack of scruples—or of research—on my part. I hope that some of my own modest modifications will be new to the veteran trickster, but to claim originality for them would be like blowing rings in a smoke screen.

B. T.

Contents

4

Shuffles—Fair, False, and Fancy

5

The Build-Up

6

How to Force a Card

7

Special Decks

8

Sudden Stuff

9

Gamblers' Sleights

10

Subtle Stuff

11

Flourishes

12

More Impromptu Tricks

How to Do Tricks with Cards

Chapter 1

The Magic Key To Magic

"To be swift is less than to be wise."

ALEXANDER POPE

ONCE UPON A TIME, I saw a pup get on an escalator.

He approached it curiously, and then patently decided that he wanted nothing to do with the silly thing. But he was intrigued, in spite of himself. Gently urged, he put his front feet on the contraption. He thought that by keeping his rear quarters on *terra firma* he could retreat if his nerve failed, but he was pulled aboard. He tried to stop his forward motion by sitting down; but the steps rose under him, more or less goosing him to his feet. Thus, he was carried along.

I hope that the newcomer to card trickery who has bought this book will find the subject as compelling—if he will forgive the obvious ineptitudes of the comparison—as that pup found the escalator. I hope that, having taken the jump, he will find himself carried smoothly along—but in an upright position and ready to take a step or two for himself.

The art of informal card trickery is, of course, a branch of conjuring; but there are signs that it is beginning to untie itself from the apron strings of its mother art. It has a tendency to follow its own paths because the pack of cards lends itself to subterfuges that are not adaptable to other forms of legerdemain. And recently card magic has attracted more and more devotees who have little interest in cumbersome deceptions with hats and rabbits and nickel-plated apparatus.

In fact, more than one magician of my acquaintance prophesies that a card-trick craze is about to sweep the nation—a nation, it might be pointed out, with a bridge deck in every home and love of mystery in every heart. Of course, one overestimates the prevalence of one's own predilections. The collectors of shrunken heads no doubt believe a shrunken-head fad imminent—and if there are people who like gooseberry ice cream, they probably expect Walgreen's to make it their next week-end special brick. But it would be useless for you to argue with one of my miracle-mongering friends. He would reply by performing the latest "coincidence" trick.

You would select a card from a shuffled deck and he would select another card from another deck. The two cards would—through a strange coincidence—turn out to be duplicates! When you asked the trickster to reveal the secret to you, so that you could fool the people who are coming over for gin rummy tomorrow night, he would say, "See? You are getting the bug already!"

It is fun to be mystified. It is twice as much fun to mystify people. Aside from the satisfaction of being able to entertain, you will find a thrill in meeting the tacit challenge of your spectators—the I-dare-you-to-fool-me look in their eyes—with an apparent miracle. And you'll get a kick out of being considered an expert in the intricacies of the "Devil's Bible."

But it has always been hard for a newcomer to crash the party. For one thing, you can't collect tricks as you might dance steps—merely by seeing them performed, because no good card magician ever exposes a trick to his audience. All there is to a trick is its mystery. To expose it is to destroy it and to reduce the status of its performer from that of a wizard to—well, just a guy who's read a book on card tricks.

While it is perfectly ethical to explain tricks in a book of

18

instruction, the sad fact is that the few readily available books on card trickery are almost invariably disappointing to the beginner. They are haphazard collections of tricks and sleights. The sleights seem sheer jugglery and many of the tricks seem too simple to attempt. When he does try one out, the novice is liable to find that he doesn't fool anybody.

Now, the fault of these books is less in their selections of tricks than in neglect of certain aspects of technique. Aside from a few lead-pipe cinches, card tricks are duds except in the hands of a performer who knows not only how they work, but also how to work them. The best tricks are simple; they require technique to make them subtle.

This brings us to what I call the magic key to card magic:

The success of a trick does not depend upon the cleverness of its secret. It depends upon the cleverness of its performer.

Approach the subject with this view and you will have boarded the escalator to expertness.

The technique of deception divides naturally into two branches:

1. PHYSICAL TECHNIQUE, which includes the ruses that accomplish certain basic actions such as getting a card to the top of the deck, switching one card for another, keeping the cards in a certain order while shuffling, etc. Some of the old magic books devote plenty of space to physical technique; but they make a difficult study of it. Some of the most deceptive sleight-of-hand, however, is *not* difficult. You can become well-grounded in this branch of technique without months of arduous practice. The important thing is to learn to conceal physical technique by making use of

2. PSYCHOLOGICAL TECHNIQUE. A knowledge of this branch of technique is absolutely necessary to the successful card trickster. Yet, it is glossed over in the books on card magic, or it is omitted entirely. It is the means used to conceal physical technique by making the spectators

19

see a trick as you want them to see it. In its more positive aspect it is the dramatization of your actions in a way that builds a mere trick into a minor miracle.

Misdirection is part of this psychological technique of deception. It is the science of controlling not only the spectators' eyes, but also their minds. It is this phase of magic that attracts so many doctors, lawyers, teachers, and other people who have a particular interest in the way the human mind works. I once heard a psychiatrist—who was also an excellent card trickster—say, "Through his attention to misdirection, the magician develops a knowledge of certain peculiarities of human thought that surpasses anything to be found (on these certain peculiarities) in psychology books." Misdirection is easy to learn—once you get on the right track. We will consider examples of it in the next chapter.

So, this book has been designed to teach you three things: 1. physical technique; 2. psychological technique; 3. tricks. You will learn all three more or less at once. You will see how physical and psychological technique are related and how they apply to tricks. Then you will see how to give a trick an exciting plot and build it into a fascinating mystery. After that, your education will become more and more a matter of putting into practice what you have read; so there will be more and more tricks. I hope, unless you are already a seasoned wizard of the pasteboards, you won't succumb to a temptation to jump from trick to trick at the expense of the material on technique. That would defeat my whole purpose and you would be learning the hard, slow way. And you would probably come to the conclusion that the tricks in this book—among which are some of the best close-up card mysteries in existence—aren't much good. Let me repeat. If you are going to fool anybody besides your near-sighted aunt, you have to know how to present a trick—not just how it works.

There are two or three sleights in this book that aren't easy. They have been included because you should be familiar with them as part of your general knowledge of card magic. There is no difficult sleight in this book that is indispensable—in fact, you will be better off at first if you skip the fancy-Dan stuff and concentrate on the easier tricks and sleights until you can do them swiftly and efficiently.

Of course, even easy tricks require practice; but practice is fun. The rule is:

PRACTICE A TRICK UNTIL YOU CAN DO IT AUTOMATICALLY. That's only common sense. You aren't going to look like much of a wizard if you have to stop to remember what comes next. The best plan is to work out all the tricks in each chapter; then pick out one or two to learn thoroughly. Later, when you want new ones, you can go back and perfect others.

You've come to the end of your first lesson without having learned your first trick—that comes in the next chapter. But begin that chapter with the desire not only to learn tricks but to learn to be a trickster—which, as you now know, is quite a different thing. If you will do that, your repertoire won't be restricted to those few sure-thing tricks, most of which are as stale as the jokes about fountain pens that write under water. The whole field of card magic will be open to you.

Chapter 2

Misdirection

"Oh, what a tangled web we weave,
When first we practice to deceive!"

SIR WALTER SCOTT

THERE ARE MANY KINDS of card tricks. Some are based on secret manipulation of the cards, others on tricked decks, mathematical principles, or special apparatus. But, as I have already suggested, the modern magician looks on the mechanical aspects of a trick as of secondary importance.

He considers every trick *an exercise in applied psychology*.

Let's see what happens when a person watches a trick: He sees the performer go through a series of actions which seem to lead to a certain result. When the magician reveals an entirely different result, the spectator can't explain what he has seen on any natural grounds. Of course, he knows there *is* a natural explanation; but he is unable to discover it.

Obviously, some of the magician's actions were different from what the spectator thought they were; or, the magician performed one or more actions of which the spectator was not aware. But the spectator cannot look back and see what must have happened. He is baffled because as far as he can see every action was what it seemed and the magician had no opportunity to add secret actions.

You see, the *trick takes place in the mind of the specta-*

tor. To bring about that trick, you must control his thoughts to the extent that he sees no possibility of camouflage or concealment as you handle the playing cards—even though you actually get away with murder. The methods by which you control his thoughts are called, as I said earlier, *misdirection*. There are certain general rules of misdirection, but it is also a system of specific subtleties that have been found to be effective. The best way to get a grasp of misdirection is to analyze an example of it. So we come to our first bit of card trickery—

A False Cut

Suppose that you want to keep the deck in its exact order, yet appear to cut it. The obvious thing to do is to break it into two packets, as for a fair cut, but to assemble it just as it was in the first place. If you do just that without benefit of misdirection, your cut won't get by one person in ten. Apply misdirection and you can practically fool yourself.

The first application is negative: *Do not call attention to what you are doing*. Go through the actions *casually*, as if they were a mere formality and not at all important. Emphasis creates suspicion. If you announce, "I shall now cut the cards," the spectators will get the idea that there is something important about this cut and they will watch you as they'd watch Lucretia Borgia making sandwiches.

You should be talking about something other than your actions. And do not look at your hands as you make the cut. The eyes of the audience tend to follow your eyes; and to look at an action is to emphasize it.

Still—this is the second bit of misdirection—cut the cards *openly* and without haste. Hold the deck at the tips of your fingers and expose as much of it as possible. If it seems plain to the spectators that you are not trying to conceal anything, they relax their suspicions.

Casualness and openness are obviously not enough. So now you get really subtle. You take advantage of a com-

23

mon human weakness—the tendency to observe badly, or, more precisely, the tendency to forget promptly what has been observed. You do this by handling the cards in a certain way.

Hold the pack in your left hand, palm upward, between the top joint of your thumb on one edge and the tips of your fingers on the other edge. With the thumb and fingers of the right hand, cut a packet of cards off the bottom of the deck and draw it clear. Give this packet a quarter turn, bringing its face toward your body. Tap its end two

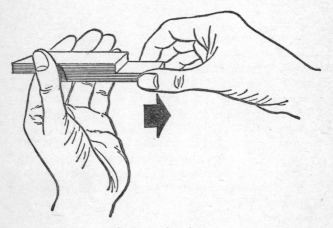

Beginning the False Cut

or three times against the end of the upper packet, as if to square the cards. Don't do this for longer than a couple of seconds—*that is long enough for the spectators to forget whether the packet in your right hand came off the top or the bottom*. After all, since you are doing all this casually and openly and giving the impression that the cut is of little importance, why should they bother to remember?

However, you want to create an impression that the right-hand packet came from the *top* of the deck. So you pass this packet *over* the cards in your left hand and lay it on the table. The spectators see you put down a packet of cards with the exact motion you would use if you cut it off the top; subconsciously, they decide that is where it came from.

Finally, your right hand returns for the other packet and places it on top of the one on the table.

If you will try this false cut, you will realize at once how deceptive it is. If you are reading this book in a place where no cards are handy, use two books of matches or two other flat objects to represent the halves of the deck. You can see now that it is almost imperative to have cards in your hands when you are learning tricks from a book. Even the simplest manipulations are hard to follow unless you perform them as you read.

Do you see how the physical and psychological techniques of deception are related? The physical actions of the trickster are determined largely by psychological considerations. Let's do another exercise in misdirection—and learn an easy subterfuge that you will use in many tricks.

The Simple Pass

After a card has been chosen and returned to the deck by a spectator, it is often necessary to bring that card secretly to the top. That is the purpose of the simple pass.

Let's suppose that you have fanned the deck and that a spectator has chosen a card. Before he returns the card, hold the deck in your left hand in the following manner: The left edge of the deck is against the base of the thumb and parallel to the life line in your palm. When you grip the deck by bending the fingers over it, the little finger should be at the lower right corner.

Now lift off about half the cards with the right hand and invite the spectator to return his card to the top of the packet in your left hand. You have merely cut the deck so that the card can be returned to its center. But as you replace the upper half of the deck on top of the chosen

25

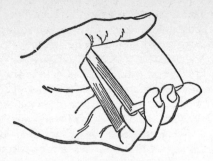

Holding a Break for the Simple Pass

card, insert the *tip* of your left little finger between the two portions of the deck. This is the means by which you secretly keep track of the selected card. Pressure on the cards with the left thumb will keep them flush except at the corner where the finger tip is inserted. Naturally, you keep this corner toward your body—away from the spectators.

For a moment you keep your right hand over the cards, fingers on front end and thumb on rear, squaring the pack. However, there is another reason for this. It may occur to the spectators that you somehow mark a place in the pack. So you keep your right hand on the cards in order to distract suspicion from your left. The suspicious spectator is reasoning something like this: "He could be keeping a break in the deck. Why is he holding the cards in two hands? Yes, he must be holding a break with one of his right fingers." So you now take your right hand off the cards and smooth your hair or flick an imaginary fly off the end of your nose. At the same time you turn your body slightly so that there is no danger of revealing the break at the lower right corner of the deck. Your spectator now reasons, "Oh, he's taken his hand away. I guess he wasn't marking a place with it after all."

Some spectators will not suspect that you are holding a break at all, but there are always one or two suspicious souls. When you have performed for an audience a bit, you will realize that these characters think very much as I have suggested above. You will notice a relaxation of their scrutiny as soon as you remove your right hand from the cards.

Now, your problem is to get the selected card to the top without anybody's realizing what you are doing. Turn your left hand to bring the deck into position for the old-fashioned overhand shuffle. Immediately take the cards above your little finger into your right hand and shuffle them onto the face of the deck. I don't have to tell you to

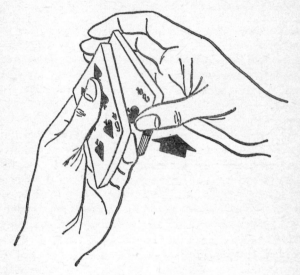

Beginning the Simple Pass

do this casually and openly. Give the impression that the shuffle is an automatic action, that you hardly realize what you are doing. Talk about something else. You may say something like this: "For centuries magicians and mind-readers have been aware of an inexplicable relationship between the human mind and the fifty-two playing cards. So I am going to ask you to think very hard about the card you just selected. Rule every other thought out of your mind. . . ." And so forth.

The spectators' minds are occupied with what you are saying. There is no room in them for suspicions about what you might be doing. They register only what you obviously *are* doing—shuffling the cards. The chosen card seems lost.

As a general rule of misdirection: *When you are engaged in an action which you don't want the spectators to question, TALK.* The inexperienced trickster is inclined to fall silent when he is making a vital manipulation. This pause is fatal. It not only allows the spectator to center his entire attention on your action, it also emphasizes this action and invites suspicion. So, talk. The more entertaining your patter, the better misdirection it is. To say something that will have your spectators *laughing,* while you unobtrusively swindle them, is about the best misdirection there is.

I hope that you are beginning to feel the fascination of card magic when it is approached from the psychological angle. It is a lot more fun to feel that you are fooling people by your own cleverness than by merely exhibiting tricks that work themselves. There are a very few foolproof tricks that would be reasonably effective in the hands of a backward child with an advanced guilt complex. But the master of misdirection can make perplexing mysteries out of stunts that would be obvious in the hands of the uninitiated.

You are now ready for your first trick, an easy, mystifying one.

The Card on the Wall

EFFECT: A card is secretly noted and returned to the deck. After shuffling, the performer shows a thumb tack and appears to insert it into the deck. He shows that the top card is not the chosen one. He flings the cards against the wall and they scatter to the floor—all except one, which remains stuck to the wall with the thumb tack. And it is the selected card!

METHOD: Have a card selected and get it to the top by means of the simple pass. Show the thumb tack and say that you are going to drop it into the deck. Hold the deck in the crotch of your left thumb and tip its end back toward you so that no one can see exactly where the tack goes. Your right fingers catch the edge of the top (selected) card and bend it backward. Place the tack directly behind it, point toward you. You then press the top card with the left thumb so that the point of the tack pierces this card. Keep the left thumb in front of and against the point of the tack and no one will see it.

Your right thumb goes to the end of the pack nearest your left little finger and separates the top two cards. With your right fingers at the opposite end of these two cards, lift them and show them as *one* card. Say, "This doesn't happen to be your card on top, does it?" The answer will be no, because the spectator sees the face of the second card. Return these two cards to the top. Throw the deck so that it strikes the wall flatly behind the projecting tack point. The weight of the deck will drive the tack into the wall and the selected card will be held there.

Sometimes it is more fun to make the card stick on the ceiling, but the throw is a bit trickier.

Chapter 3

The Palm, the Slip, and the Pass

"What witchery is this?"

SHAKESPEARE

A SLEIGHT, OR MOVE, is a swift, efficient manipulation of which the spectator is unaware. It is a mechanical action, concealed or disguised by misdirection.

The simple pass is an example of a sleight. We are now going to examine three more basic sleights—two easy ones and a toughie—and learn simple tricks utilizing them.

You already know that before you show a trick to anyone you should practice it until you can do it automatically. Here are some more general rules which will contribute to your success as a truly mystifying card magician. To be precise, the last three rules are corollaries of the first; so I present them as follows:

Rule: *Don't let your audience get ahead of you.*

This means: (A) *Don't tell them what you are going to do before you do it.*

(B) *Don't do the same trick a second time during a performance.*

(C) *Don't use the same sleight more than two or three times during a performance.*

Let's briefly examine each of these rules.

If you let your audience know, for instance, that you

are going to make a selected card leave the deck and appear in the center of a book, they will recognize those actions that are steps in getting the card out of the pack and into the book. If they don't know what your goal is, they will see nothing suspicious in those actions. They will react to the casualness and openness (remember?) with which you perform, and they will not remember your actions in detail; so they won't be able to figure out the trick by reviewing it in their minds. There is a big difference in looking for a specific thing as you see a trick performed and looking for the same thing only in memory.

For a similar reason, do not repeat a card trick for the same people the same evening. When you get a request to "do it again," you can be sure that the requester has been fooled—but good. Be firm—if necessary, be stubborn. The best answer I know is to begin another trick, throwing out the impression that you have given in and are repeating the last one. The spectator wipes off his bifocals and peers. Expecting one climax, he gets another, and is more perplexed than ever.

The danger in using the same sleight too often is that your onlookers will begin to wonder why you repeat your actions so exactly. Take the simple pass, for example. You have the card returned by breaking the deck, then you shuffle—somewhat unorthodoxly (with card faces toward the left). Repetition will create suspicion that there is ulterior purpose in this sequence of actions.

If you are new to card magic, stick to these rules for a while. You will soon be able to sense what your audience is thinking at every stage of a trick! If you make an exception to a rule then, you will know if you are suspected, and you can throw the audience off the track with a false shuffle or some other interpolation.

The first sleight you will learn in this chapter must be as old as the art of card magic. It is an extremely simple one, although it may seem complicated on paper. The secret of performing it indetectably is to emphasize *naturalness* as you practice it.

There is a big difference between holding a card in your palm so that your audience can't see it and holding it so that they do not suspect it is there. First, let's consider merely how to hide a card efficiently: Hold it lengthwise in your hand with the fingers curved inward so that the card presses tightly against the flesh. The exact position of the card will depend upon the size and shape of your hand. Approximately, the lower edge should follow the longitudinal center of your little finger. One end should extend from just above the top joint of the little finger to just below the top joint of the forefinger. The lower index corner of the card should press into the fleshy base of the thumb, *not* into the crotch of the thumb. The fingers, of course, are held close together.

There is one dangerous thing about palming; if you move your hand around at all, it is very easy to get it at an angle that will give your spectators a flash of ink and cardboard. A flash is all they need. So you must be conscious of the exact angle your hand makes with the spectators' line of vision during every second you have a card palmed.

As I've already suggested, naturalness is the secret of indetectable palming. I once knew a magician who had crooked fingers that would not fit tightly together; but his movements were so logical and the attitude of his hands so natural that he had no trouble getting away with palming. But he was a past-master of misdirection—don't let his example make you careless about keeping your fingers together.

The best way to attain naturalness in palming is to observe the exact attitude of your hand when you have nothing in it. Then imitate this position as nearly as possible with fingers close together and a card palmed. Keep your thumb parallel with your fingers. Do not make the common error of sticking it up like a flag on a farmer's mailbox. When you are reading or listening to the radio, hold a card

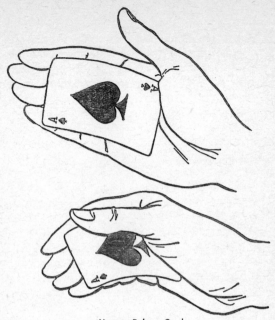

How to Palm a Card

palmed for several minutes at a time. This painless exercise will do a lot to give your fingers a relaxed, natural attitude while they conceal a card.

You are now ready to learn how to steal a card off the deck into the palm. You are given three methods of doing this. Learn all three if you like, or choose the one that seems most *natural*.

From now on as you read this book (or almost any book on card tricks), remember that the "top" of the deck is always the surface which is the back of the first card that would be dealt in a game—*even when this surface is turned downward*. The "bottom" is *always* the face of the last card.

If you possibly can, have cards in your hand as you read the following instructions.

METHOD ONE: This is a neat, fast steal. Hold the deck

in your left hand, thumb at the center of left edge, tips of fingers evenly spaced along right edge. Now turn the deck so that the top surface is to the right. Turn your body slightly to the left so that the back of your right hand will be toward the spectators as this hand approaches the cards. With the tips of your right fingers push the top card forward three-sixteenths of an inch.

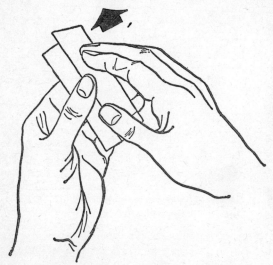

To Palm a Card from the Deck—First Method (A)

Next, the right fingers go to the front end of the deck and appear to square up the cards. Secretly, they press lightly on the protruding end of the top card and spring it neatly into the right palm. This springing-and-palming action requires practically no motion of the right fingers, which are already curved into a natural palming position and are held at an angle of about sixty degrees to the pack.

The instant the card is in your palm put your right thumb at the rear end of the pack and lift it out of your left hand. This is the misdirection that covers the palming action. Apparently, you have merely transferred the cards from one hand to the other.

METHOD TWO: Hold the cards in the crotch of the left

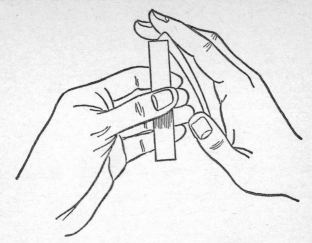

To Palm a Card from the Deck—First Method (B)

thumb with the thumb resting on top as if you were going to deal. Square up the deck with your right fingers at the end as in the first method. Push the top card a quarter of an inch to the right with the left thumb. Press on the upper

To Palm a Card from the Deck—Third Method (A)

right corner of this card with the right little finger tip. Get the left thumb out of the way and the top card will spring into your right palm. Cover this action as you did the previous one—by taking the deck into the right hand.

METHOD THREE: Hold the deck at the left finger tips as in the first method, with these differences: (1) The deck is reversed and the bottom card is to the right. (2) The tip of the left first finger is not at the edge of the deck with the other three fingers but against the back of the top card.

Turn your right side toward the audience. Place your right fingers over the end of the deck, hiding the cards for a second. Push the top card forward with the left first finger. Draw the rest of the pack toward your body by bending your left wrist. At the same time, press the top card into your right palm with the left first finger.

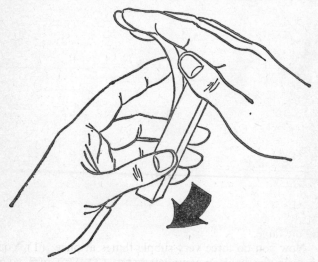

To Palm a Card from the Deck—Third Method (B)

There is more motion in this method of palming than in the previous ones. Here is a neat way to cover it with a natural action: As soon as the card is in your palm, take the deck between your right thumb on its bottom and your right fingers on its top. Straighten your left wrist and immediately return the deck to your left hand but this time with the back of the top card toward the audience. This makes the whole palming action seem to be one of simply reversing the deck.

The first trick you will learn that is based on palming is about the most un-subtle trick in this book as far as method goes. It depends almost entirely upon naturalness in palming. That's why I've put it here: it is an excellent exercise. If you will master it (it can be made a very mystifying trick), you will be well on the road to mastering the whole technique of deception.

The Card in the Book

EFFECT: A card is selected and returned. The magician asks the spectator to pick his card out of the pack, but it is not there. It is found in the pages of a book that has been lying in plain view on the table.

METHOD: Get the selected card to the top by means of the simple pass. Palm it by your favorite method.

Show the bottom card, holding the deck in your left fingers. Drop your right hand, card palmed in it. The most natural position is not at your side but in front of you, below your belt. Your right fingers may rest lightly against your body. Once your hand has been dropped to this position, do not move it around. Even a minor adjustment of its position may draw attention to it. Keep attention centered on the bottom card, which you are showing.

Ask the spectator, "Is this your card on the bottom?" When he answers negatively, say, "Suppose you run through the deck and remove your card." Lay the deck on the table.

Now you do three very simple things at once. (1) You pick up the book in your left hand. (2) You turn your right side squarely to your audience. (3) Raise your right hand to the back cover of the book. The tips of your right fingers are against the cover; the right thumb is on the front edge of the book to open the pages.

Crack the book near the center. Let the front section of pages fall open until they are almost parallel to the floor, but keep the back section at an angle of sixty degrees to the floor. Place your right hand squarely in the opening, your right thumb at the edges of the pages to the left. It pulls these pages to the right onto the others. As you withdraw your right hand from the book, release the palmed card. The right fingers at once seize all the pages between the covers. Face the spectators, lowering the book. Riffle the pages until the card is suddenly disclosed among them.

The actions with the book take place without hesitation. You appear merely to pick up a book and open it, getting all the pages into the right hand. There is no need to wait until the spectator has run through the entire deck before you bring the trick to its climax. The fact that you let him take the cards into his own hands is enough to demonstrate that his card is not there. If he is a suspicious soul as well as a pokey one, you can let him go on looking after the trick is over.

I hope you spend some time with The Card in the Book. It is an extreme example of how deception depends upon *you* and not upon the method of the trick. It will be good for your morale.

Here is another trick based on palming. A startling one —with a subtle method.

The Brainbuster

EFFECT: The magician fans the top few cards of the deck and the spectator selects one by merely thinking of it. This card vanishes from the deck and is found in the magician's pocket.

METHOD: Fan the top seven or eight cards, but hold one card behind the fan in a position where it can't be seen. Ask a spectator to think of one of the cards and to remember at what number it lies from the top of the deck. Square the deck, and ask the spectator to tell you the number. Suppose he says five. In reality his card is sixth because there was one more card in the fan that he didn't know about. You deal five cards from the top of the deck, laying aside the fifth. Say, "That should be your card. Turn it over."

As he does so, palm the card that is now on the top of the deck. It is the card the spectator thought of. Ask the spectator to name his card. Suppose he says it is the five of hearts. You say, "Oh, it couldn't have been. I put the five of hearts in my pocket ten minutes ago."

Shove your right hand into your trousers pocket and bring out the palmed card.

The Slip

(Also known as The Top Slip and as The Slip Change)

Hold the deck on edge across the bumps at the bases of your left fingers. The top of the deck is to your right. The left fingers bend inward against the back of the top card. The left thumb holds the upper edge of the deck.

The right hand now grips the deck with fingers at outer end, thumb at inner. It breaks the deck at the center, opening it like a book. It now lifts off the top packet; but as it does so the left fingers press against the top card, quickly slipping it to the top of the lower packet.

To cover this sleight, turn your left side toward the

The Slip

spectators. Lift the upper packet away with a circular motion of the right hand, revolving the right thumb outward. At the same time, revolve the left thumb inward. When the slip has been made and the packets are clear, point to the bottom card of the right-hand packet with the left forefinger. Make some remark about this card. You have appeared to do nothing more than cut the deck into two packets, exposing the bottom card of the top packet.

You will find this sleight neat and easy, and to perform it will give you the feeling that you are becoming a very slick character. Two tricks based on the slip follow.

Cut Your Card

EFFECT: A spectator secretly notes a card and returns it. After shuffling the pack, the magician (that's you) requests a spectator to shove the blade of a knife (or anything else that's handy) among the edges of the cards at whatever point he pleases. The magician cuts at this point and reveals that the spectator has found the noted card by sticking the knife blade just above it!

METHOD: Get the selected card to the top with the simple pass. Hold the deck in position for the slip. Have somebody slide a knife blade among the edges of the cards. Break the deck at this point, ask him to withdraw his weapon, and perform the slip. Point to the face of the top packet and say, "This is where you inserted the blade, right?" Extend the other packet and let him turn the top card.

The Prophet

EFFECT: The trickster writes something on a slip of paper, which he folds and gives to somebody to hold. Another person breaks the deck with a knife blade and peeks at the card below this break. The first spectator opens the folded paper and reads aloud, "Bill Moore will select the ten of hearts." Which turns out to be correct.

METHOD: To make a person take the card you want him to take, while he thinks he has a free choice, is *to force a card*. As you have guessed, you force a card in this trick by means of the slip.

You begin by fanning the cards and studying their faces for a moment, quite openly. All that you really do is make a mental note of the top card. Write the name of this card on a piece of paper, fold it, and hand it to a spectator to hold. Have Bill Moore stick a knife blade into the edge of the deck. Execute the slip. Have him look at his card. Let him shuffle the deck—a gesture which makes no difference to the outcome, of course, but which gives a halo of fairness to the proceedings. After suitable build-up, tell the first spectator to read the message you gave him.

The (Old-Fashioned) Pass

This venerable sleight was once indispensable to the card magician. It has now been largely replaced by easier methods. It demands hours and hours of practice. If you don't think it's worth the time, skip it—you can be an expert card trickster without it. Skill in manipulation is no index to skill in deception. And the latter is better entertainment. I'd rather watch the kid next door *mystify* people with the Twenty-one Card Trick than see Ringling Brothers' gorilla deal seconds from a stack of wheatcakes with his toes as a feat of pure, undeceptive jugglery. . . . Of course, if you like tough stuff and have set out to become a hotshot ticket-tripper, fine. Don't let me talk you out of anything.

The pass (also called the shift, the two-handed pass, and *sauter la coupe*) should be done with flash-bulb speed. There is an old rule that you shouldn't make use of it until you can do it sixty times in one minute. (That means you have one second to complete each pass and get your fingers into position for the next.) Even so, the sleight is not entirely invisible when done with the hands stationary. It must be covered by some natural movement, or—better yet—by directing attention away from the cards.

The purpose of the pass is to cut the deck secretly at a place where your little finger holds a break.

Hold the pack in the crotch of the left thumb as if you

were going to deal. The top joint of the thumb extends onto the deck. The last three fingers curl over the right edge onto the back of the top card. The forefinger curls up over the front end, which nestles into its second joint near the right corner. With the right thumb, break the deck at its inner end and insert the left little finger until the top knuckle is just out of sight.

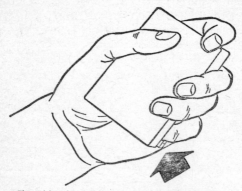

The Old-Fashioned Pass—Position of the Left Hand

Cover the pack with your right hand, fingers at front end, thumb at rear. The right forefinger is just to the left of

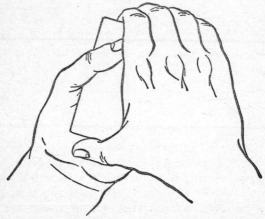

The Old-Fashioned Pass—Position of the Right Hand

center and the right thumb is directly opposite on the inner end of the pack.

This right thumb and finger grip the lower half of the cards—the packet below the break. The other three fingers of the right hand are relaxed. The packet above the break is gripped between the left little finger and second and third fingers.

In spite of all this "gripping," don't let me give you the idea that you should hold the pack tightly. Dainty does it. Just imagine that you found the cards in the day room at Molokai.

So far you have been just getting into position. This is a good place to warn you that in actual performance you must never be obvious about getting set for something. Don't telegraph your punch.

Comes now the pass itself.

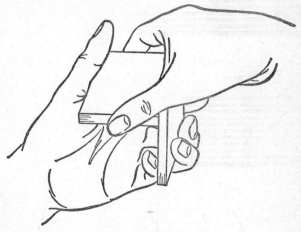

The Pass Half-Completed

With your left fingers, draw the upper packet to the right until it is at a right angle to, and clear of, the lower packet. At the same time, lower your left hand a bit, pressing downward on the left edge of the lower packet with your left thumb near its base. This pressure causes the lower packet to pivot in the crotch of the thumb as if it were

43

hinged there. Draw the original upper (now lower) packet into the left palm with the left fingers and up against the bottom of the original lower (now upper) packet.

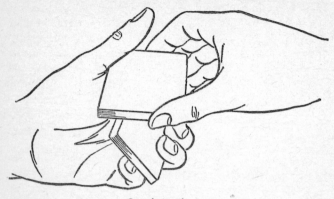

Completing the Pass

Remember, the left hand does all the work. The right hand merely holds its half of the deck (between forefinger and thumb) and remains motionless. You will know when you have the action just right: the packets will spring around each other and neatly (and silently) into place.

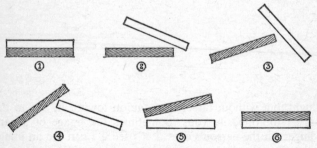

The Old-Fashioned Pass—End View of Deck as Halves Change Places

The most common use of the pass is to bring a selected card to the top of the deck. You secretly insert your little finger above the card after it has been returned, and in a flash you pass it to the top.

Covering the Pass

When you have learned to do the pass neatly and reasonably fast, you can begin to work on the problem of covering it. Your solution will depend largely on your own mannerisms. If you are a person to whom such motions are natural, you can make the pass as you move your hands to one side in a gesture; or you can bring the pack back toward your body with a rather large motion of the arms after you have had a selected card returned.

But be sure that your covering motion is not itself a giveaway. If your audience thinks, "He did *something*—I don't know what!"—your cover is a flop.

Probably the best plan is to keep your hands still and make sure that the people are looking somewhere else. For instance, ask the spectator who has just returned his card to stand up. (Provide a plausible reason for this, of course.) As he gets to his feet and eyes turn toward him, that's your moment.

Or ask a spectator to pick up some object you're going to use in the trick you're doing. Seize your opportunity when everyone becomes interested in that object.

At the Card Table, the Pass Can Be Covered Perfectly— a fact not appreciated by many magicians. Here's how to do it: Allow the outer edge of your right little finger to touch the edge of the table a little to your left. The motionless right hand and the table top combine to screen the action of the left hand as it makes the pass.

Another Method: Having had a card selected and returned, lean back in your chair. Hold the deck in plain sight, but without directing attention toward it. Say to the spectator opposite you, "Sometimes the image of a card lingers in the person's eyes. Let's see if I can see an image in your eyes." Lean forward and peer into his eyes. Place your right elbow on the table and lean on your right forearm, which coincides with the table edge almost to the tip of your little finger. Do the pass. Say, "No, I don't see an image. Just a gleam." Straighten up and proceed with the trick.

The Herrmann Pass

Here's another pass—a somewhat easier one. It is called the Herrmann pass because Alexander Herrmann, the great magician of another day, is said to have delighted in baffling fellow prestidigitators with it.

In the past few years, the Herrmann pass has blossomed into great popularity with close-up card tricksters. Many clever variations have been the result. A favorite follows.

You seem to do nothing beyond turning over the pack to expose the bottom card, but you accomplish an invisible cut.

Hold the pack face down on the left hand. Your left thumb is parallel to and against the left edge; it extends about an inch beyond the front end of the deck. The top joints of your last three left fingers rest against the right edge of the deck; they do *not* curl up onto the top card. The *very tip* of your left little finger holds a break above the card you wish to bring to the top. The top joint of the forefinger rests lightly against the front end of the deck at the index corner.

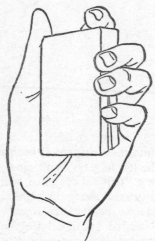

Holding a Break for the Herrmann Pass

Your right hand covers the pack. Your right forefinger

goes to the extreme left corner at the front end; its tip touches the tip of the left thumb. Your right thumb is directly opposite at the inner end. Take hold of the cards above the break between your right thumb and first two fingers. Let your right third and fourth fingers rest lightly on your left forefinger. Now turn your right hand a little to the right until the lower right corner of the top card touches your right thumb near its base.

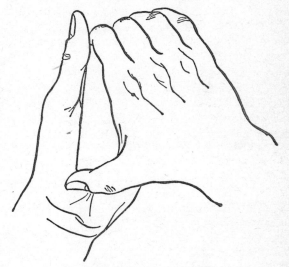

Ready for the Herrmann Pass

Hold the deck loosely. Allow the break to extend along the length of the right edge. Insert the tips of the left two middle fingers into it. Carry the lower packet slightly to the right with the left fingers. Don't move the left thumb. Thus, you make a "step" about three-quarters of an inch in width, which extends along the right side of the deck.

Press down on the back of the lower packet with the tips of the left second and third fingers. Keep pressing until the lower packet stands up on its right edge. Its opposite edge pushes against the bottom of the upper packet, causing the latter to pivot against the left thumb.

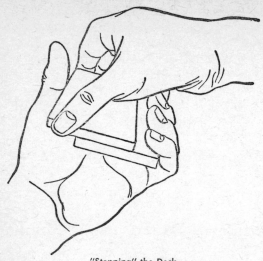

"Stepping" the Deck

When the packets are clear of each other, *extend* the
right middle finger and *bend* the forefinger. This snaps the

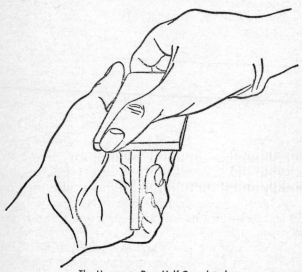

The Herrmann Pass Half-Completed

right edge of the upper packet downward. The original upper packet is now to the left of and roughly parallel to the original lower packet. Press the two packets together with your left thumb, and turn the deck over to expose the bottom card.

The success of the Herrmann pass is a matter of timing rather than speed. The transposition of the packets must be hidden in what appears to be the one motion of turning over the pack.

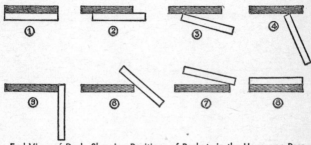

End View of Deck, Showing Positions of Packets in the Herrmann Pass

The following trick is based, as I have described it, on the regular pass. You can easily substitute the Herrmann pass if you wish.

The Hypnotic Aces

EFFECT: The magician places the two red aces together in the center of the deck. He places one of the black aces on the top and the other on the bottom of the deck. He shows the audience that the aces are exactly where he says they are. He then shows that a red ace has jumped to the bottom. Another red ace is on the top. The two black aces are in the center. The magician then explains that he has hypnotized the spectators and that they only imagine that the aces changed places. He fans the deck again and shows that the aces are in their original positions.

METHOD: Fan the deck (backs toward you) to show that all four aces are just where you said you put them. Place the right forefinger on the face of the upper red ace. As you square the cards you will find it easy to break the pack at this point and insert your left little finger between the two aces. Make the pass. Show that a red ace is now on the bottom, another on top, and fan the deck again to show that the two black aces are now in the center. Repeat your previous actions, getting the little finger between the black aces. Make another pass, snap your fingers to un-hypnotize your victims, and show that the aces have again changed places.

You won't be able to perform this trick without a whale of a lot of practice, of course. Don't attempt it until you are absolutely sure of your ability to perform an indetectable pass.

Probably you have noticed that in this trick you violate the rules about not repeating sleights. You get away with it because when you reach the first climax the spectators think the trick is finished. They relax their attention. Before they realize that there is more to come, you have performed the pass again and accomplished the second part of the trick.

In his fine book on conjuring, *Learn Magic,* Henry Hay gives a deceptive version of this four-ace trick in which the pass is done *four* times.

There are so many tricks that require your getting a chosen card to the top of the deck that you should know more than one method, even if you don't feel like learning passes. So, for good measure, here are several easy ways of sneaking a card to the top.

Bridge and Shuffle

When you cut the pack to have the selected card returned, hold the upper portion of the cards with your fingers at one end and thumb at the other. Quickly and secretly bend this half of the deck by pressing its ends forward so that the centers of the cards are bowed back toward your palm. Do this as you extend the lower part of the deck and the card is returned on it. Replace the top half and immediately take the deck in your left hand with fingers on the bottom and thumb on top. Hold the cards

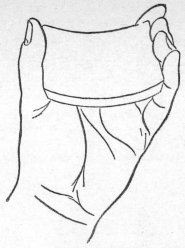

Bridging Half the Deck

just firmly enough to eliminate the bridge you made in the upper half of them.

Casually show the pack from all angles. Square it by thumping its edges on the table. When you release the pressure of your thumb and fingers, the bridge will re-

The Bridged Deck

appear. You can easily cut to it—even without looking at the cards. Just to be different, do a riffle, or dovetail, shuffle this time instead of the overhand shuffle that you do in the simple pass. Make sure that the top card of the lower packet is riffled last and falls on top of all the others.

The Short Card

Prepare one card by trimming one thirty-second of an inch off its end. Return this card to the deck, square the edges, and you will find that you can always cut to this short card by riffling the ends of the cards with your thumb. It makes a sort of snap when it falls, and there is a tendency for the riffling action to stop at this point.

Have a card selected and peeked at. Riffle the pack with your thumb, casually break it at the short card, and have the spectator return his card at this point. Square the edges of the deck and set it on the table for a moment. Pick it up, riffle, cut to the short card. The chosen card is on the face of the cut; when you have carried the cut, it will be on the bottom of the deck.

To get a card to the top by means of the short card: Riffle and break the deck at the short card. Press lightly on the back of this card with the tip of the right thumb. Draw off the top packet toward your body. The downward pressure of the right thumb is just enough to pull the short card along with this packet. As soon as the card is a half inch to the rear of the lower packet it will pivot on the rear edge of this packet and spring against the

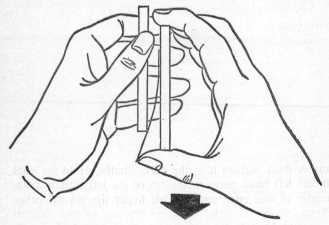

Springing the Short Card to Bottom of Upper Packet

bottom of the cards in the right hand. The slightest wiggle of the right thumb will shove it into a position where it may be held securely. Have the selected card returned under it. Now if you riffle and cut, the selected card will be brought to the top.

The Crimp

The term *crimp* has two different meanings for magicians. It means a card with one corner bent slightly up or down. And it means a single card bent along one of its axes in a manner comparable to that called a *bridge* when applied to more than one card.

A card crimped in either fashion may be readily cut to.

To apply the first kind of crimp, extend the deck face down in the left hand and invite the spectator to return his card by shoving it among the ends of the others. But press down on the top of the deck with your left thumb so that the card can't be pushed all the way in. It is perfectly natural for you to come to your assistant's aid and shove the card flush for him—or appear to. Place your right middle finger tip on the end of the card at the left corner. Place your right thumb on the lower left corner of the deck. Squeeze. You'll find that you always shove the card in crooked; its lower right corner will bump against your left third finger. Bend this corner upward with a quick thrust of this finger—a motion that is covered by the right hand. You have inflicted a crimp that may be easily spotted and cut to. But for maximum effect, give the pack a thorough shuffle first.

The second kind of crimp is best applied, not to the selected card itself, but to a card which you contrive to get above the selected card, as you did the short card. As good a way as any to crimp a card is to palm it—rather hard. Return it to the deck. Shuffle. Hold the pack in the left hand between the tip of the left thumb at the center of one edge and the left finger tips on the other. Better move the little finger to the end of the deck to prevent a cascade. Now reduce the pressure of the thumb enough to allow some of the cards to fall into your left palm. Look at the face card of this cut. The chances are good that it's the crimped card. After a few tries you'll develop the knack of cutting to the crimp every time.

Card in Position to be Crimped. Lower Right Corner Should be Bent
Upward with Left Third Finger

You can see how to make use of this: Have a card
selected. Extend the deck in the left hand, letting it break
at the crimp, and have the card returned at this point.
Square the deck. Cut to the crimp whenever you feel like

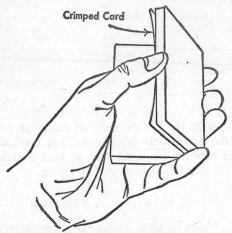

Crimped Card

Cutting to a Forward-Crimped Card

it. The selected card will be on top of the lower packet.

In the next chapter, you will learn a one-hand cut—an easy flourish that will be useful in connection with a card crimped in this manner.

NOTE: To behave as described above, the card must be crimped *forward;* that is, palmed with its face outward. If you crimp it the other way, you'll always cut it to the top of the lower packet.

The Double Cut

You've had a card selected and returned and are holding a break above it with a tiny ridge of flesh at the tip of your left little finger. Place the last three fingers of your right hand on the front end of the deck, thumb on the rear end. Bend your right forefinger and press its tip down on top of the top card. Lift off about three-quarters of the pack with the right hand, *pressing against the rear end of the cards with your right thumb to retain the break*. Press your right forefinger against the top of this packet to keep the break from showing along its sides.

Immediately lower the right-hand packet and shove the cards in the left hand on top of it. Your left fingers slip under the deck to its right edge. Your left little finger immediately takes up the break again. Cut again—this time to the break, bringing the chosen card to the top.

Do you see the subtlety of cutting *twice?* The spectator thinks something like this: "He's cutting the deck. I wonder if he's somehow marked the place where I returned my card and is cutting to it. Maybe that's my card he's cut to the top. Nope, he's cutting again. If that was my card he's lost it. He has the deck all mixed up now."

That's the way people think, son. They confuse easily. And when they are confused they sit back and trust the guy who confused them. Ask any politician.

Having a Selected Card Returned

You've learned to have a chosen card returned to the center of a cut pack—a procedure that makes it easy to get your little finger tip on top of the card. There are other, perhaps better, ways of accomplishing this.

One is to have the card shoved into the end of a squared deck—as you did when you crimped a corner. Press down on the cards with the left thumb to keep the spectator from shoving his card flush. You shove it in crooked so that its lower right corner protrudes from the right side of the deck (see The Crimp). As you square up, press downward on this protruding corner with your left third finger. This will make a break into which you can insert the little finger tip.

Another method is to hold the pack in the left hand, spreading the cards into the right for the spectator to insert his card among the others. When he has done so, get your left finger tips on the face of the card above the one just returned. As you close the deck into the left hand, bend the left fingers. You'll find that you have made a break that can be easily transferred to the tip of the pinky as you square the edges.

Chapter 4

Shuffles—Fair, False, and Fancy

"Patience, and shuffle the cards."

MIGUEL DE CERVANTES

The subject of shuffles is not the digression that it may seem at first. You will be able to make the tricks in the chapters that follow even more mystifying if you know something about it.

In the first place, you should be able to handle your props gracefully. No matter how puzzling your tricks are, your skill will be discounted if you shuffle like a deacon with a sore thumb. So let's begin with an ordinary, fair shuffle.

The chances are that you already do some version of the dovetail or ruffle ("riffle" to magicians) shuffle deftly enough. However, if you have to have something to rest the cards on, you'll find it more convenient to be able to dovetail in your hands. Here is the correct way:

Break the deck into halves. Each hand grips an end of a half with the two middle fingers pressing the cards upward against the palm. The packets are held at an angle: Their centers should be directly under the bases of the forefingers. These fingers themselves shouldn't be doubled up on top of the packets; they should extend over the edges. The thumbs are at the inner ends of the cards. If you have the position, one lower corner of each half of the deck will be against a second joint of a middle finger and the opposite lower corner will be at the base of a third finger.

The thumbs bend the ends of the cards upward (if you find them difficult to bend, you are not gripping the lower ends tightly enough with your middle fingers). The thumbs riffle the cards and let them dovetail.

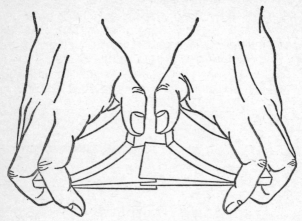

The Dovetail Shuffle

You can finish the shuffle by simply shoving the cards together, or you can spring them together with the pretty little flourish that is so common among bridge players. To do this (in case you don't already know how), place the thumbs firmly on the two packets where they are

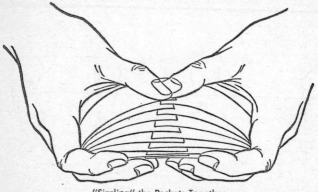

"Sizzling" the Packets Together

joined. Bow the cards by bending downward the ends held in the fingers of each hand. Relax the fingers, extending them parallel to the floor to catch the cards, but keep the thumbs firmly on the apex of the bow. Slightly lessen the tension by moving the hands apart a fraction of an inch and the pasteboards will "sizzle" into a neat pack.

The dovetail shuffle is often used by magicians when they want to keep a few cards in order on top of the deck. They merely remember which of the packets they are shuffling is the top half of the deck, and they make sure that the last cards of this packet are riffled after the last cards of the other packet.

False Dovetail

This is a little-known method of keeping the entire pack in order, though you appear to dovetail shuffle. To perform it you must be able to dovetail in your hands.

Hold the two packets in position for dovetailing with the top part of the deck in the right hand. Shuffle as described above, but instead of letting the cards dovetail along their entire width, join only the corners of the packets—the corners away from your body. Swiftly pivot

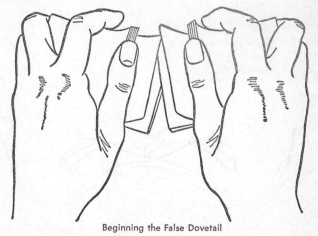

Beginning the False Dovetail

the packets at this joint, turning their outer ends away

59

from your body and toward each other. Continue this motion until the knuckles of your forefingers meet and the packets slip apart. Immediately reverse the turning motion, slightly raising the inner end of the right packet to allow it to slide onto the left packet.

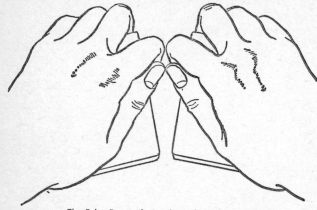

The False Dovetail—Breaking the Halves Apart

This shuffle is completely deceptive when done speedily. The audience gets the impression that the cards were dovetailed and shoved together with a little flourish. The old professor can't resist a warning, however: do this false shuffle casually, but *not* too openly. And don't repeat it too often.

We come now to the old overhand shuffle. Because many people have their own little variations of this easiest of all ways of mixing the cards, let's briefly examine it as it is done for thaumaturgic purposes.

Hold the pack in the left hand with its edge across the bases of the fingers. The left finger tips are against the face of the bottom card and the thumb is on the back of the top card. The right hand cuts a packet from the bottom of the deck, taking it between the thumb at the inner end and the fingers at the outer end. It lifts this packet up and over the other and then makes a series of up-and-down motions into and out of the left palm. Each time the right-hand packet is in the palm, the left thumb

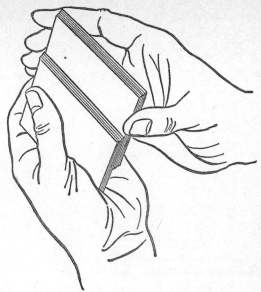

Beginning the Overhand Shuffle

presses against its top and draws one or more cards onto the left-hand packet.

The Gambler's Shuffle

This shuffle is a standard sleight with almost all expert card tricksters. It is easy to do and appears perfectly fair. Yet it will keep the top half of the cards in order.

Hold the cards in position for the overhand shuffle. Cut about half the cards off the bottom of the pack with the right hand and lower them into the left palm. The left thumb presses against the top card of this packet and draws it off, *but in such a way that it projects over the end of the other packet about a quarter of an inch toward your body*. The rest of the cards in the right hand are now shuffled on top of this card, but so that they are square with all the other cards. When you have finished this first part of the shuffle you have one card projecting slightly between the mixed cards and the undisturbed

61

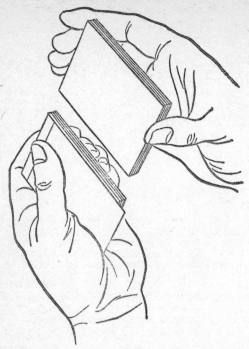

The Gambler's Shuffle—Showing the Injogged Card

section that you want to keep in order. In the terminology of the legerdemain-iac, this card is *injogged*. If it projected over the outer end of the pack, it would be *outjogged*.

Your right thumb presses the injogged card slightly to the left, making a break between the shuffled and un-shuffled sections. Your right hand at once cuts off about three-fourths of the deck. That is, it takes all the cards below the break and about half the cards above the break. The right thumb retains the break while the left thumb draws off the cards above it a few at a time. You appear to be continuing your shuffle. When the last card above the break is in the left hand, simply drop the whole right-hand packet on top of the shuffled cards.

The gambler's shuffle should be performed quite briskly, but neatness and rhythm are more important than speed.

It is almost impossible to detect, even if you use it again and again. It is easy to learn, and I suggest that you perfect it even if you pass up every other shuffle in this chapter.

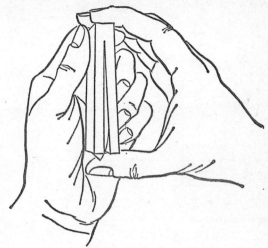

The Gambler's Shuffle—Cutting to the Injog

The Running Cut

Hold the deck in the left hand with the top joint of the thumb on one edge and the finger tips on the other. The right thumb and forefinger undercut (cut off the bottom) about three fourths of the cards, holding this packet by its edges near the end. As the right hand draws its cards clear, the left thumb and fingers release the top quarter of the deck and it falls into the left palm. The right-hand packet is now moved directly over the left-hand packet and immediately drawn away again, leaving a small section of its top cards gripped between the left thumb and fingers. This section is dropped on top of the cards in the left palm. The right hand returns with its packet and the action is repeated. In this way, a rapid series of cuts is performed until the cards in the right hand are exhausted.

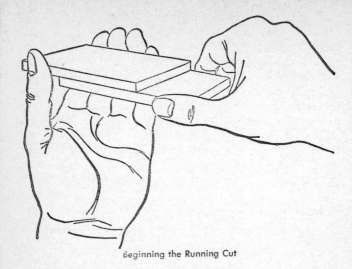

Beginning the Running Cut

The False Running Cut

Begin exactly as for the fair running cut: undercut a packet with the right thumb and first finger and drop the remainder of the cards into the left palm. The right-hand packet is moved in above the left-hand packet as before, but this time the right thumb and first finger grip

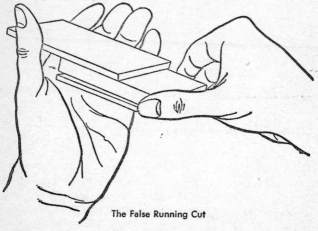

The False Running Cut

this lower packet and carry it away under the upper. At the same time, the left thumb and fingers draw off a few cards from the upper packet and let them fall into the palm to take the place of the ones you have spirited away. The right thumb and first finger hold a break between the two sections of cards they grip. They continue leaving a few of their top cards at a time in the left hand, just as in the fair running cut. When they come to the break, they drop the whole packet on top of the cards in the left hand. Hence, the shuffle is completed without disturbing the top part of the deck.

The false running cut is not nearly so difficult as it reads. Wade through the above instructions with cards in hand and you will have a valuable addition to your repertoire of false shuffles.

The False Triple Cut

This is a good false cut to use whenever you are performing seated at a table. You appear to make a somewhat elaborate triple cut. In reality, you assemble the cards in their original sequence.

Beginning the False Triple Cut

The pack lies on the table before you, its length parallel with the edge of the table. Pick it up with your left thumb and forefinger on opposite edges near its left end. Hold the cards a few inches above the table. With right thumb and forefinger, undercut a small packet, holding it by the edges near its right end. Place this packet on top of the other cards, but don't release it from the right hand. With the tips of your right thumb and middle finger, cut a packet off the original top of the deck and withdraw it

The Second Step in the False Triple Cut

under the cards your right hand already holds. Hold a break between these two packets. With a brief sweeping motion of the right hand to the right, allow the upper packet to fall to the table. Place the left-hand packet on top of it. Finally, add the packet which remains in your right hand. You have assembled the bottom, middle, and top sections of the deck in order, though you seem to have mixed them.

The One-Hand Cut

This startling flourish seems to have been acquired at the expense of long practice; but if you will give careful attention to the details of its execution, you can learn it

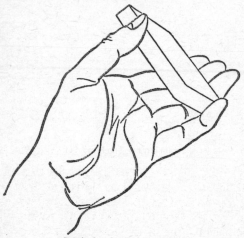

Ready for the One-Hand Cut

in a few minutes. Perform it nonchalantly at the bridge table, or during a routine of tricks, and you will add greatly to your reputation for manual dexterity.

Hold the deck by its edges in your left hand at the extreme tips of the thumb and fingers. Your left palm is upward and the cards are parallel to the floor. The first three fingers press against one edge of the deck, the middle finger at the exact center of that edge. The tip of the thumb holds the opposite edge, just to the left of center. The little finger tip rests against the ends of the cards—its purpose is to keep them from cascading to the floor.

The thumb and fingers allow about half the cards to drop in a packet into the palm. We will call this *packet A*. The cards still held between thumb and finger tips are *packet B*.

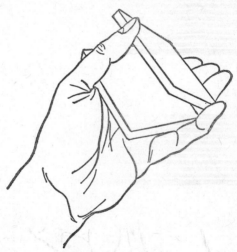

Beginning the One-Hand Cut

The first finger leaves its position at the edge of packet B and bends downward until its tip is against the bottom card of packet A. It pushes packet A upward, pivoting it in the crotch of the thumb, until this packet is against the thumb and forms a right angle with packet B. The thumb releases packet B and holds packet A upright. The

67

first finger bends downward and out of the way, letting packet B fall into the palm. Packet A falls on top to complete the cut.

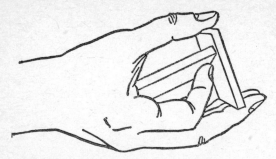

Raising Lower Packet with Forefinger (As Seen in Mirror)

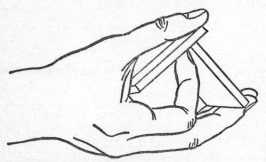

Completing the One-Hand Cut (As Seen in Mirror)

Don't worry if the packets slip and wobble at first like a couple of kites in a high wind. You'll soon be able to control them perfectly. When you can, try.

The One-Hand Shuffle

Proceed as with the one-hand cut up to the point where the two packets are at right angles to each other. Raise the first finger until its nail touches the bottom of packet B, holding this packet in position while the thumb releases its grip. The thumb breaks packet A to let six or eight cards fall off its bottom into the palm. The first finger allows packet B to fall on top of these cards; then this finger goes to the bottom of the enlarged packet and raises it with the help of the middle finger—whose tip presses against the back of the top card. The thumb drops a few more cards from packet A, and packet B is again lowered on top of them. The manipulation is continued until the cards in packet A are exhausted.

The One-Hand Shuffle (As Seen in Mirror)

This one-hand shuffle has value beyond looking pretty. It is really a false shuffle: it does not disturb the order of the top section of the deck.

A false shuffle or cut, while it depends upon a certain amount of misdirection for its success, is in itself a piece of misdirection. By casually doing one at the right moment, you convince your audience that you can't know the position of a single card—even though you have the exact order of the pack written on your cuff!

Some tricks depend almost entirely on false shuffles. For instance, any trick with a pre-arranged deck would be about as subtle as a sash-weight, if the deck were not shuffled as part of its presentation.

Being able to false shuffle convincingly opens to you any number of tricks where you deal yourself a winning hand in an exhibition card game. For instance, you can stack an interesting poker deal, as follows: 9D, QH, 10S, 6S, AH, QC, JS, JH, 9C, AC, JD, 10D, 9H, 8D, AS, 10C, 9S, 8C, 7D, AD, KH, 8S, 7H, 10H, 2D. Having introduced the stacked deck in an unsuspicious manner, false shuffle, false cut, and deal five hands. The result will be four hands containing straights while you, the dealer, hold four aces. But you aren't through yet. As you examine each hand in turn, get the high card of the straight to the bottom of each five-card packet and the ace of hearts to the bottom of your own hand. Return the hands to the top of the deck in any order. False shuffle and false cut. Again deal five hands and this time you will get a royal flush.

To stack four perfect bridge hands you need only arrange the deck in four-card sequences of suits in order. After false shuffling, you may allow anyone to cut.

Chapter 5

The Build-Up

*"The magic of the tongue is the
most dangerous of all spells."*

EDWARD BULWER-LYTTON

The word "showmanship" is apt to suggest Barnum
and Bailey, Hollywood, publicity men, and perhaps Frank-
lin D. Roosevelt. But every day of our lives most of us
engage in a certain amount of showmanship, which is no
more nor less than the art of pointing-up the most appeal-
ing features of whatever we have to offer. Billy Rose is
a showman; but so is every gal who wears an uplift bra.

The appeal of card tricks is in their mystery. When we
apply showmanship to them, it is as a means of building
up that mystery. So, as we will use the word, showmanship is a part of the psychological technique of deception.
Misdirection, by concealing what really happens, is a
means of fooling people. Showmanship is what makes the
difference between mere trickery and *magic*.

For a clue to the best way to build up a little mystery
into a big one, let's look at the technique of the mystery
story writer. He creates a puzzle by having somebody
murdered by an unknown hand. But he doesn't let it go
at that. He builds his puzzle into an absorbing mystery
by stimulating the imaginations of his readers. He sets
his story against a mysterious background. He introduces
a legend about a hideous monster that roams the country-
side, a cult of devil-worshipers, or at least eerie lights on

the moor. The murderer may turn out to be some meek character with no eerie light about him except the shine on his pants; but by introducing elements that are mysterious in themselves, the writer vastly increases the grip of his mystery.

The successful card trickster follows the same formula. He builds his bare trick into a gripping mystery by chattering about some awe-inspiring subject such as hypnotism, thought waves, spiritualism, extra-sensory perception, and so on.

Remember the Card in the Book? There is nothing particularly clever in the means by which the trick is accomplished: you have to rely upon skillful misdirection to get away with it. Let's suppose you have practiced it and can get the card into the book without arousing suspicion. Your spectators sit back and ask themselves, "Now, how did he manage that?" You have puzzled them but have not really created much of a mystery. The trick needs a few puffs of showmanship to blow it up. Try pattering something like this:

"There is an old superstition that the positions of the cards in the deck are often determined by strange factors other than shuffles and cuts. As you know, many people consult fortune-tellers in the belief that the cards arrange themselves into esoteric patterns that symbolize the past, present, and future of the person who cuts them. Now, I have been experimenting with this ability of the cards to hop around, and I have had some interesting results. I have found that I can not only make a card move around in the deck, but that under certain conditions I can even make it leave the deck and materialize elsewhere. At first, the trouble was I could never tell where it would turn up. Finally, I discovered that it always went to a place that approximated the conditions of the deck—an environment where it lay flat, pressed between other flat objects. The pages of a book, for instance, are an ideal place for the rematerialization of a card. . . ."

Don't be afraid of sprinkling the dream-dust on too thick. If you can make your audience visualize funny little men under the table, so much the better. You have made the trick more than just an action no one detected. You have given some substance to the mystery and have presented, so to speak, an illustrated fairy tale.

A mystery in a story is not at all gripping, however—no matter how spooky its background—if the action is slow and stops cold in places. The same is true of a card trick. So let's touch on some additional points which come under the heading of showmanship and which will increase the mystery of a trick by adding to its all-around entertainment value.

1. Perform at a rhythmic, rapid pace. Move from one phase of a trick to the next without hesitation. Don't stop the action while you talk. Keep it moving right along with your tongue.

2. Be clear. Of course, there are parts of every trick that must be concealed from the company. But be sure they are aware of all the other parts. If the guy over by the cocktail shaker gets the impression that you just hand a spectator a card instead of allowing a free choice, he is not going to be exactly startled when you reveal the name of the card.

3. Emphasize those of your actions which are *fair*: the free choice of a card, the fact that a spectator is allowed to shuffle or cut, the fact that the deck is not in your hands at the climax of the trick, and so forth. This emphasis is both good misdirection and good showmanship.

4. Make the climax as startling as possible. Once again, let's consider the Card in the Book. You don't assert, "The card is now in the book." You say, "The pages of a book, for instance, are an ideal place for the re-materialization of a card." At the same time you riffle the pages and let the spectators *discover the card for themselves*.

Are you ready to try out your showmanship? Each trick in this chapter is readily adaptable to presentation as an experiment in telepathy, a feat of mind-reading, a spirit manifestation, or some such intriguing nonsense. Just give your imagination a free rudder and work out a line of chatter that fits your own personality and makes a bare plot into a mystery.

While the tricks that follow are good material on which to try out your showmanship, they have also been selected for another reason: they are all in the "impromptu" category. They will be especially valuable to you because you can perform them any time, any place, with a borrowed pack of cards. Guard the secrets of these tricks carefully. Remember, to expose a trick is like pricking a balloon with a pin—there just isn't anything left. Don't give in—even to the little-number-with-the-big-eyes—when your spectators beg you, as they will, to "tell us how you did it." If you do, you can be sure of one thing—they will be disappointed.

The Spectator Takes Over

EFFECT: A spectator shuffles the pack and cuts it into halves. He keeps one half; the magician takes the other. Each places his half behind his back and shuffles again. The spectator then peeks at the top card of his packet. The deck is assembled. The spectator places it behind his back, reverses one card, and shoves this card anywhere into the deck. He brings the cards around and spreads them into a row on the table. The magician doesn't touch the cards, but the spectator finds that he has located the card he peeked at. He finds that he inserted the reversed card directly above it.

METHOD: When the spectator has shuffled the deck and given you half of it, make some remark about the importance of creating a situation where it is impossible for you to know the position of a single card. So, you say, you will both mix your cards a bit more—behind your backs. You only pretend to mix your packet, however. Here is what you actually do: Reverse the bottom card. Also reverse the card just below the top card.

Have the spectator note the top card of his shuffled packet. Emphasize the fact that he need only peek at an index and that you can't possibly know what the card is. Then place your packet on top of his. Be extremely careful not to flash the bottom card, which is reversed and which goes immediately above his selected card. Ask the spectator to hold the deck with his thumb on its top (this is an un-obtrusive way of making sure he doesn't forget which side is which when he gets the cards behind his back). When the cards are out of sight, tell him to move the top card to the bottom of the deck. When he does this, he unknowingly brings a reversed card to the top. Following your instructions, he turns this card over and shoves it into the deck. Actually, it goes in right side up, though he thinks he has turned it face up. When the cards are spread on the table, he naturally thinks that the reversed card which you have contrived to get next to the selected one is the card he shoved into the deck.

This is an easy, clean-cut trick. It is especially effective when presented as a feat in controlling a person's muscles right down to the fine point where you cause him to insert a card exactly where you want it in the deck. Incidentally, one time in fifty your assistant will shove the top card between his selection and the reversed card above it. About all you can do in such a case is shake your head sadly and opine that he has something wrong with his kinesthetic sense, because he appears to have missed by one card.

The Spelling Trick

EFFECT: A spectator selects a card and returns it. The magician shuffles. He asks the spectator to name his card. The magician immediately spells the name of this card, dealing one card from the top of the pack for each letter. He turns the last card face up—it is the one he spelled.

METHOD: Get the selected card twelfth from the top. An easy way to do this is to count eleven cards into the right hand as you spread the deck to have a selection made. Have the card returned under these. Another way is to bridge the top eleven cards before you start. Still another is to have the card chosen from twelve dealt onto the table; casually gather the other eleven on top of it.

The rest of the manipulation occurs in your head. With a little practice—maybe as much as half an hour's—you'll have no trouble spelling any card in the pack in twelve cards.

In the heart and spade suits, the four, five, nine, jack, and king spell in twelve letters if you spell them thus: k-i-n-g-o-f-s-p-a-d-e-s. Turn the card on the *s*. The ace, two, six, and ten spell in eleven letters; so turn the card after the *s*. The three, seven, eight, and queen are reduced to eleven letters by leaving out the "of"—spell only number and suit.

In clubs, the four, five, nine, jack and king spell in eleven letters. Three, seven, eight, and queen spell in twelve. Ace, six, and ten require only ten letters. If one of these is the selected card, show the top card with the remark, "I want you to see your card is not on the top of the deck"; then boldly put this card on the bottom. Or speak the words "ace" and "of" after you have spelled them, dealing a card for each. Spell the two of clubs d-e-u-c-e.

The ace, two, six, and ten of diamonds spell neatly in eleven letters if you leave out the "of." The three, seven, eight, and queen require that you spell diamonds without the *s*. You get away with this by announcing, "First, I will spell the number of your card; then the suit. Your card is a queen, you say? Q-u-e-e-n. And it's a diamond. D-i-a-m-o-n-d." Turn the card on the *d*.

All this is easier to learn than you think at first. Practice by taking twelve cards in your hands; put each on the bottom of the pile in turn and spell it. The Spelling Trick is always baffling and has been one of my favorites for years. I do not need to point out that it will *not* bear repetition.

The Four Ace Trick

Some variations of this trick are so elaborate and require so much effort for the spectator to follow that they make a rather dull dealing routine out of what is essentially splendid entertainment. So let's learn a speedy, simple version.

EFFECT: Four aces are laid face down on the table. Each ace is covered with a small packet of cards. The aces are openly placed on top of each packet. The faces of the cards are shown as this is done. Each ace is now laid in front of its packet, and the packets are picked up. Several cards are dealt onto each of the aces.

A spectator chooses a pile and is told to keep his finger on it. The other three piles are turned over, revealing that the ace has vanished from each. The spectator turns over his pile—it contains all four aces!

METHOD: Place the four aces face down in a row on the table. Hold the pack face down in the left hand. Riffle its inner end with the right thumb, separating the top four cards. Place these on top of the first ace without letting the spectators see exactly how many cards are in the packet. Say, "I'll place a few cards on each ace," as if the exact number doesn't matter. Place four cards on the other aces in the same manner. Keep talking, and remove each packet of four cards as quickly and casually as possible.

Pick up the packet to your right. Hold it face outward in your left palm, clipped securely between your finger tips and the flesh of your palm. The spectators see the top of the ace peeking over your first finger. With the left thumb, push the top card of this packet to the right. Take this card between the right thumb on its back *at the lower right corner,* and the right first and second finger tips on its face. Keep the edges of the cards in the left hand square. Push the next card into the right hand in the same way, taking it under the right thumb on top of the first card. Then, the third card. But the fourth and fifth cards—the ace and the card above it—you transfer as one card. Shove the lower right corner of this card under the right thumb. As you withdraw the left fingers, bend back the upper left corner of this double card to expose the face of the ace. Say, "The ace goes on top of the others." Let the double card snap into place and immediately square the packet. Place it face down on the table.

Do exactly the same with the next two piles of cards. Make sure that the spectators think there is an ace on top of each pile; but don't emphasize this point to the extent that you arouse suspicion. When you come to the fourth pile, don't transfer the cards singly from one hand to the other. Simply remove the ace from the bottom and place it

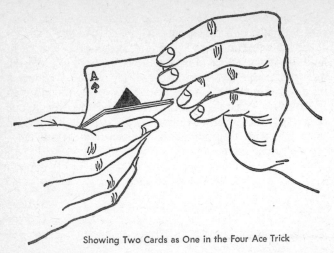

Showing Two Cards as One in the Four Ace Trick

openly and fairly on top. When this pile is returned to the table, it goes to your left of the others.

Now slide the top card of each packet forward to make a row of single cards in front of the packets. The spectators think these are the four aces; in reality they are, from left to right, one ace and three indifferent cards. If you like, you may "accidentally" flash the face of the ace as you move it forward.

Pick up the packet on your left first. Place the others on top of it. Return the assembled cards to the top of the deck. False shuffle. The gambler's shuffle you learned in the last chapter is an ideal one to use here.

Deal one card onto each of those on the table from the left to right. Repeat until you have four packets of four cards each. You seem to have four piles with an ace at the bottom of each. The fact is that all four aces are in the left pile.

Your problem now is to force the spectator to choose this pile. Designate a spectator who directly faces you. Quickly push each pile forward an inch, beginning with the one that contains the aces. Say, "Will you please touch one of the piles?" Say this as if it doesn't matter a hoot which pile he touches.

If your timing is good and the spectator's glands function normally, he'll touch the pile *you touched first*. If he's an opium-eater, an army officer, or in the publishing business, he might touch one of the others. In that case, tell him to keep his finger on it, and say, "Now, *I'll* choose a pile." Choose the one with the aces. Keep your finger on it. Invite two other spectators each to place a finger on one of the remaining piles. Modify the trick to the extent that the aces vanish from under the spectators' fingers and assemble under yours.

The "22" Trick

EFFECT: Someone chooses a card from a shuffled deck and returns it. He then goes through the deck, dealing the first card into a hat, the next onto the table, the next into the hat, etc. When the deck is exhausted, he picks up the cards on the table and repeats the process. He does this until all the cards are in the hat except one—which turns out to be the card he selected.

METHOD: All you have to do is to make sure that the chosen card is twenty-second from the top when the spectator starts the dealing-and-discarding process.

Begin by shuffling the pack overhand fashion. Run twenty-one cards into the palm of the left hand and injog the twenty-second. You must do this in such a way that you seem to be shuffling, however, and not counting. (1) Don't look at the cards. (2) Break the rhythm of your shuffle now and then. Run seven cards rapidly; pause an instant with the right-hand cards lowered into the left palm but kept separate from the others; run seven more; ask who would like to assist you with this trick; run three; pause; run four; injog and shuffle off the rest of the cards on top of the injog.

This is all very simple to do, albeit complicated reading.

Turn the pack face down on the left palm. Place your right fingers on the front end of the cards. Lift up on the injogged card with your right thumb on the rear end, cutting this card to the face of the packet you lift off with the right hand. Shove this packet under the (twenty-one) cards in your left hand, getting a break between the packets with your left little finger tip.

So far you appear to have shuffled and cut the cards. Nothing more.

Now spread the deck to have a card drawn. First spread the cards above the break, shoving them into the crotch of the right thumb. You'll find this makes it easy to place the tip of your right first finger on the face of the twenty-first card to mark your place. Separate the cards here and have the chosen one returned twenty-second.

The spectator deals the first card into the hat, the next onto the table, the next into the hat, the next on top of the one already on the table, etc. He must deal into the hat *first* each time he picks up the packet from the table and starts over, even if the last card went into the hat.

There's a lot of dealing in this trick. Dealing can be very dull entertainment. But not necessarily. It's up to you to create interest and suspense.

For instance, choose for your assistant a man who belongs to the local Friday Night Quarter-Limit Society. Tell him you are going to test his ability as a poker player. Have him peek at each card as he deals it. Say you are going to tell by his expression when he puts the selected card into the hat. Invite the other spectators to try to catch him too. Of course, he never does put it into the hat.

That's just a suggestion. You take it from there.

Do As I Do

This is generally considered one of the finest card tricks ever conceived. Almost every card magician has one or more versions of it in his repertoire. The method I give you here is the simplest, and the best.

EFFECT: The trick is done with two decks. The spectator chooses one and gives the trickster the other. The spectator imitates the motions of the magician, shuffling the cards, cutting them, peeking at a card, assembling the deck and giving it a final cut. They then trade decks. The magician says, "You pick the duplicate of your card out of my deck. I'll pick the duplicate of my card out of your deck." They lay their cards face down and turn them over simultaneously. To everyone's surprise, the cards are the same!

METHOD: Shuffle the cards by dovetailing, so that the spectator who is imitating you will shuffle the same way. Try, without being obvious about it, to glimpse the bottom card of his deck. You'll find that most people expose the bottom card when they square up after shuffling. If you have picked a cagey customer, however, glimpse the bottom card of your own deck and *trade with him*. Simply say, "Now you take my deck and I'll take yours."

Lay your deck in front of you on the table. Cut to your left. Indicate that the spectator is to cut to his right. Peek at the card you have cut to (the top card of the packet to your right). The spectator peeks at the corresponding card in his deck. Say, "You remember your card and I'll remember mine." Actually, pay no attention to the card you've just looked at; it has nothing to do with the trick. Say, "Now we'll lose our cards by cutting them to the middle of their packets." Complete a cut with the *packet* on your right. The spectator imitates you, and brings the bottom card of his deck on top of his selected card. You assemble the halves of your decks. Have the spectator follow you through another cut for good measure (which makes no difference—he may cut as often as he likes) then trade decks. Tell him to pick the duplicate of his card from your deck, and say you'll pick the duplicate of yours from his deck. You pick the card below the key card that you secretly noted—and the trick is turned.

There is plenty of drama in the effect of this trick. It is an easy one to build up as a master mystery. It is a prime illustration of the contention of the best magicians that method doesn't matter a hang. Get a good *effect,* and you have a good trick. Skillfully apply misdirection and showmanship to this trick, and you have a miracle.

Kings and Queens

EFFECT: The performer places the queen of spades in his pocket. The queen of hearts is placed between the two red kings. The queens change places.

METHOD: Having borrowed a deck, run through it and pick out the two red kings and the queens of hearts and spades. Arrange these cards on the deck as follows, from the top of the pack down: the two red kings; below these, the queen of hearts; next, an indifferent card, and finally the queen of spades. The spectators don't know about the indifferent card between the queens.

Lay the two red kings face up on the table. Turn the next card, the queen of hearts, and hand it to a spectator. Ask him to insert it face up between the kings. As he does this, secretly get your little finger tip under the top two cards. Lift this double card and casually show it as one—the queen of spades. Keep it slightly in motion as you show it.

(There is endless debate among card conjurers over the best way to show the top two cards as one. In spite of all the elaborate methods that have been suggested, each performer develops his own pet, and that is what I'm leaving you to do. Lift the double card by the lower right corner, or by its ends, or snap it off the pack by seizing the lower index corner—work out the way that seems to you the most natural and open and casual.)

Return the double card to the top of the deck, keeping a tiny break under it. Remove the single top card as if it were the queen and shove it into your trousers pocket without showing its face. Say, "We'll put this one in my trousers pocket and forget about it." Say "this one"—not "the queen of spades." Once it is safely in your pocket and you have performed some subsequent action, you can name it —but not until then.

Pick up the three cards on the table with the right hand. Call attention to their order: "Red king, queen of hearts, red king." Turn them face down and place them on top of the deck, where you still have your finger tip under the queen of spades. Square the edges of the cards and then move the top *four* cards to the right. Move them about two-thirds of the way across the deck and hold them there with the left thumb on the back of the packet and the left finger tips on its face.

Your audience must think that this packet contains only the red kings and the queen of hearts. Remove the top card and show its face, keeping the packet square. Say, "Red king." Turn it face down and shove it on the bottom of the packet of four. Turn the next card. Say, "Queen of hearts." Turn it face down and put it on the bottom. Do the same with the next card, which is the other red king.

Say, "Remember the order—red king, queen of hearts, red king." As you say this, again transfer three cards one at a time from the top of the packet to the bottom, *but don't show their faces.* You have now got the queen of spades between the red kings. Square the packet with the deck. Ask somebody to name the three top cards. He says, "Red king, queen of hearts, red king."

Lay the top three cards face down on the table and say, "Turn them over and see if you're right." As he does so, you have a golden opportunity to palm the top card.

The queen of spades is revealed between the two red kings. Your right hand immediately goes into your pocket and brings out the palmed card—the queen of hearts. Bring it out at your fingertips—and bend it backwards to take the shape of your palm out of it.

This is an adaptation of a trick popularized by that human encyclopedia of card magic, Rufus Steele. For his version, see *Fifty Tricks* by W. F. Steele.

Chapter 6

How to Force a Card

" 'Tis Hobson's choice—take that or none."

THOMAS WARD

THE ABILITY to determine a spectator's choice of a card is a precious secret of the wizard of the pasteboards.

You have already learned a neat force—the slip. Because there are many tricks that require forcing, and because the subject is an interesting one, we are going to delve deeper into it.

You will find that the key to successful forcing is to give the impression, without saying so, that it is *impossible* to influence a spectator's choice of a card. Aside from that observation, there is little of a general nature that I can say about forcing. Each of the forces that follow embraces its own psychological subtlety.

The Regular Force

You spread the cards, passing them from hand to hand, and give the spectator an apparently free choice; yet, you force a card. This method requires a good deal of practice but it's worth it. It is not absolutely certain, but when you become skillful at it you'll be successful ninety-nine times out of a hundred.

The card to be forced is on top of the deck. Cut it to the center but place the upper half of the deck on it about half an inch to the right so you can keep track of it. Spread the upper part of the deck, passing the cards from the left hand

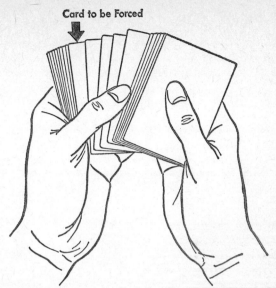

Card to be Forced

Ready for the Regular Force. Cards in Right Hand Should Be Spread

to the right, until about four cards remain above the one to be forced. At this moment, and without stopping the passing motion, extend the deck toward the spectator. The rest is timing. You'll find that with the average person you'll just about have time to pass four cards and that he'll take the fifth. Quite often you'll find a person who'll reach for the fourth card, in which case pull it quickly to the right and push the fifth into his fingers. And then there are people who reach and stop. They put their fingers close to the deck and then decide to wait a moment longer. These are easy victims—just push the fifth card into their fingers as if you think they are reaching for it (rather, you push the whole pack forward at the instant the fifth card comes into prominence). You'll find that you can do this in a way that will arouse no suspicion whatever.

Finally, there are the warped souls with no faith at all in their fellow man. They will make a quick grab near the top or bottom of the deck in an effort to foul up the proceedings. They are hard to beat, but it can be done. The best way is to shove a card from near the top or bottom at them as if it were the one you wanted them to take. Usually, this act will make them hesitate. You withdraw the card at once, saying, "Oh, you needn't take that one if you don't want it." In the meantime you have kept track of the card to be forced and you begin all over again. But this time arrange to pass your card into your right fingers sixth instead of fifth, because these characters are likely to sit and watch for a moment in a further effort to be as ornery as possible. Whatever you do, don't let this type of spectator irritate you. Take his elaborate efforts to make your work difficult as an indication that he really has a lot of respect for your ability as a prestidigitator.

If you fail to force a card, don't let anyone suspect that something's gone wrong. Have the spectator return the card, get it to the top by your favorite method, and perform some simple trick such as Cut Your Card (Chapter 3). Then try the force again on a new subject.

It will take you some time to perfect the timing necessary in this force and to acquire by experience the knowledge of what a spectator's fingers are going to do. An excellent way to practice is to try to force a card every time you have a selection made, even though the trick doesn't require a force.

The Bridge

This is another force that isn't 100% sure, but when it works it is the most effective of them all. You place the pack on the table, ask a spectator to cut and peek at the card below his cut. What could be more fair?

Remember the "bridge and shuffle" method of getting a card to the top (Chapter 3)? The bridge is an old gambling dodge, and you use it just as the gambler does—to get the cards cut where you want them cut. Have the card to be forced on top. Undercut about half the deck, bridge it, and put it on top. *A very slight bridge is all that is necessary.* Place the cards on the table and invite a spectator to cut. Try to select a spectator who has cut during a previous trick and who cuts with his fingers on the *sides* of the deck.

If he cuts that way, the chances are excellent that he will lift off the bridged half of the cards.

Three Pile Force

Get the card to be forced second from the top. Deal three piles of about four cards each onto the table, dealing one card to each pile in turn. The card to be forced will be on the bottom of the center pile. Ask a spectator to touch any pile. He will nearly always touch the center one. Tell him to peek at the bottom card, and your force is completed.

If he touches one of the other piles, however, you can still force your card. Suppose he touches the one on the right end. Say, "Turn that pile face up. Now touch another." If he now touches the center pile, say, "Leave that one face down, and turn the remaining pile face up." If he touches the pile on the left, simply tell him to turn it face up. Thus, you have a face-up pile on either side of the center pile, which is face down. Ask the spectator to peek at the bottom card of this pile, then to reverse one of the face-up piles and slip it under the face-down pile. Finally, have him shuffle, etc. Needless to say, all the time you are going through this rigamarole, you take the attitude that you are trying to make things as hard as possible for yourself and that that is the sole purpose of such a complicated method of choosing a card.

The Count-Down Force

The card to be forced is on top of the deck. Ask a spectator to name a number between one and ten. Suppose he says seven. Say, "I want you to take the deck, count down that number and secretly note the card that lies there. Get the card exactly at that number. I mean—like this." Quickly count seven cards, reversing them, to illustrate to the spectator what he is to do. Replace the cards on the deck—the card to be forced is now seventh. Quickly false shuffle or false cut. When he counts to the seventh card he will get the one you want him to get . . . Simple? . . . You'll be surprised at the smart people it will fool!

The Touch Force

This is an easy, sure-fire method. You pass the cards from the left hand to the right. You ask a spectator to touch the back of a card. You cut at that point, raising his card so he can note it.

The card to be forced is on the bottom. Hold the cards in the left hand and push the bottom card a quarter of an inch to the right as you begin to pass the cards into your right hand. Keep your hands close together. When the spectator has touched a card, cut at that point but as you raise the upper half of the cut, slip the bottom card onto its face by pressing against this card with the right fingers. Turn the right-hand portion of the deck toward the specta-

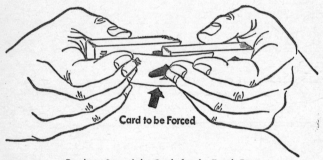

Ready to Spread the Cards for the Touch Force

tor, exposing the face of this card to him. He thinks it is the card he touched.

The Shuffle Force

Have the card to be forced on top of the deck. Casually begin an overhand shuffle as you ask a spectator to name a number. Suppose he says ten. Shuffle nine cards onto the top of the deck. Without hesitating, jog the tenth card so that it protrudes toward your body as in the gambler's shuffle, and shuffle off the rest of the cards on top of it. Cut to this jogged card and proceed as with the gambler's shuffle. Ask the spectator to count down to his number and note the card there—which, of course, is the one you want to force.

The number of tricks based on forcing is almost infinite. One of the best, if you don't mind a bit of preparation, is

The Card in the Cigarette

EFFECT: The magician tears a selected card into pieces and wraps them in a handkerchief. They disappear—all except one small corner. In the meantime, the performer has been having trouble getting a cigarette lighted. He tears it open to reveal the chosen card inside. The card is minus one corner—and the corner which failed to vanish is found to fit exactly.

METHOD: Prepare by tearing an index corner from the card. Dig the tobacco from the cigarette with a pair of small tweezers. Roll the card and insert it into the paper tube. Stuff a little tobacco into each end of this cigarette. Put it back into its package. Put the package into the left side pocket of your coat. Put the index corner of the card against the package in such a way that you can bring it out concealed behind the package.

Force a duplicate of the card in the cigarette (from a deck with the same back design!). As soon as the spectator has the card in his hand, lay the deck on the table. Bring the package of cigarettes out of your pocket with your left hand, clipping the corner of the card against it with your thumb on the side away from the audience. Casually extract the prepared cigarette and place it between your lips. Ask the spectator to hand you his card, which you take in your right hand and then transfer to your left, placing it between your left fingers and the cigarette package. Remove the package with your right hand, pressing against the corner of the card with your left thumb. In this way you slip the torn-off corner from behind the cigarette package to behind the card.

Lay the package on the table and immediately tear about a third of the card off one end. Place this third in front of the card and tear again, being very careful to keep the extra corner concealed behind the card. Finally, tear the card once the other way, making seven pieces of playing card in your fingers. The extra piece is toward your body, under your left thumb. Transfer the pieces to a similar position in your right hand. Borrow a handkerchief, holding it in your left hand at one edge.

Throw the handkerchief over the torn pieces, pushing the extra piece half an inch to the left with your right thumb. The left fingers now appear to grip the torn pieces through the handkerchief, but in reality they grip only this top piece. The right hand, still under the handkerchief, quickly palms the other torn pieces by holding them in the crook of the two middle fingers. Next, bring the right hand out from under the handkerchief and, keeping the palmed pieces concealed, grasp the handkerchief with the right fingers just under the single piece the left fingers are holding through the cloth. Twist this piece until it is securely wrapped; then lay the handkerchief on the table with the left hand. The spectators see the torn corner through the cloth and mistake it for the packet of torn corners.

Your right hand goes at once to your coat pocket and brings out a book of matches. Needless to say, the torn-up card is left in your pocket. Make quite a fuss about your cigarette not lighting. Then announce that the torn card has vanished from the handkerchief. Pretend to be surprised that one corner "got stuck." Rip your cigarette in half, remove the card, and hand it to a spectator along with the loose corner. Naturally, they will fit exactly.

Three Alike

EFFECT: Three different spectators select cards. At a signal from the trickster, they all name their cards at once. They all recite the name of the same card!

METHOD: Give the first spectator a free choice, but hold a break at his card when he has returned it to the deck. By means of the regular or slip force, force this same card on another spectator. Have him return it, then force it on still a third bystander. Say that each spectator is to try to name his card louder than the others. The result is quite startling.

The Telephone Trick

EFFECT: This is the well-known trick where a person

chooses a card, calls a telephone number provided by the magician, and hears the name of his card announced by the person who answers.

METHOD: The usual way of doing this stunt makes use of a code. The card is selected from a face-up deck, and the magician conveys its identity to his confederate by means of the name he tells the spectator to ask for. "Anderson" might signify an ace; "Ballard," a deuce; "Carter," a trey; "Davidson," a four, and so forth through a name beginning with the letter M, which would stand for a king. The suits are represented by four easily remembered first names such as, "Bill" for spades; "Bob" for clubs; "Alex" for hearts; and "George" for diamonds.

When the confederate, whose real name might be Elefter Zitzwitz, hears somebody ask for "Bobby Ballard," he knows the card is the deuce of clubs. "Bill Davidson" would be the four of spades, and "George Moore," the king of diamonds.

Another system makes use of duplicate lists of fifty-two names picked more or less at random. When the magician sees the selected card, he consults his list (which is on a small card) under the pretense of looking up a number. Then he says, "Call T. O. Klingerman at Berkeley 8601." The confederate has a duplicate list and sees at once that "Klingerman" means the six of clubs.

SIMPLIFIED METHOD: Merely arrange with your confederate to name a certain card. Force this card. Have your friend called by his real name.

Telephone Trick No. 2

EFFECT: A spectator selects a card. The telephone rings. The call is for the spectator. The voice on the phone reveals the selected card. The spectator is helped to a chair.

METHOD: Suppose you are at a party and your hostess asks you to do some card tricks. Say, "Sure. But I have to make a telephone call. It'll just take a moment." Call your confederate. Synchronize your watch with his; tell him what card to name, whom to ask for, and exactly what time to call. Do tricks until less than one minute before that time and then start talking about mind-reading. Say that it is just as easy to read the mind of a person ten miles away as that of a person in the same room, etc. *When the telephone rings,* extend the cards toward your victim with the invitation to take one. Stall until whoever answered the telephone returns and says the call is for your spectator. Say, "Go ahead and answer it—we'll finish the trick later. Just keep your card in your hand."

Tip: Pick the little-number-with-the-big-eyes as the person who selects a card. This is only good showmanship because it will assure you of a great big squeal when she hears the name of her card come over the wire.

Another Tip: Be sure of your force, brother.

The Magazine Test

Effect: Three cards are selected. Their numerical values are totaled and a spectator opens a book or magazine to the page which corresponds to the resulting number —if the values add up to twenty, he turns to page twenty. He then notes the value of the highest of the three cards and counts that many words in the text. He remembers the last word. The performer, who has seen neither the faces of the cards nor the page number, picks up pencil and paper and writes the word!

Method: Before you begin, note the tenth word on page twenty of the magazine. Get a ten, an eight, and a deuce to the top of the deck. Force one of these three cards by means of the regular force—you can hardly miss because any one of the three may be taken. If you are confident of the regular force, use it to have the next two cards selected; if not, use the slip or get the cards to the bottom and use the touch force. Once these cards are forced, you have also forced the tenth word on page twenty.

If you think it more effective, you may present this trick as a prediction by writing the word before the cards are selected.

Chapter 7

Special Decks

"Bait the hook well . . ."

SHAKESPEARE

WE HAVE seen that a trick is a series of actions which the spectator sees, plus one or more actions of which he is unaware. We have seen various ways of concealing these secret actions by the use of clever sleights and of misdirection. But the simplest and surest—if not the most artistic—way of keeping the spectator unaware of an action is to accomplish it before you begin to present the trick. So we have prepared decks.

The first principle in handling a special deck is an obvious one: don't let anyone suspect that it's special. Whenever possible, slyly substitute it for a deck that previous use has demonstrated to be fair. You can do this with ease. Have the "cold" deck in your right coat pocket along with a knife, pencil, or some other object that you will use in one of your tricks. Boldly shove the unprepared deck into the pocket, exchange it for the prepared one, and bring out the latter along with knife or pencil. Since this switch is made between tricks—a moment when you seem to have no reason for a surreptitious action—it won't arouse suspicion.

Most trick decks you can easily fix up for yourself. Some —such as the Svengali deck, strippers, the wide-card deck —are best obtained from a magic shop.

The Key-Card Deck

A key-card deck has one (occasionally more) card in it

that is specially prepared in a way that makes it easy for the conjuror to locate. You are already familiar with the deck containing a short card. Below are descriptions of other clever key cards.

THE NARROW CARD is trimmed at the edges instead of at the ends. It may be very easily cut to by gripping the cards at their sides.

THE WIDE CARD is a fraction of an inch wider than the other cards in the pack. If the cards are set on the table and a spectator is invited to cut, he will nearly always cut to the wide card. The advantages of this are numerous: It is easy to force a wide card or the card below it. You can allow a spectator to cut and be certain that he will cut to a stacked sequence of cards. You can have a spectator insert a selected card into the pack in a position where you can readily locate it, though you do not touch the cards during the selection or return of the card.

THE SLICK ACE is an ace which has been made slicker than the other cards; it may be easily cut to by holding the cards in one hand and squeezing top and bottom gently between thumb and fingers. Most magicians slick their aces with Simoniz, letting it dry a few hours and then highly polishing it. I find dance-floor wax even better.

With four slick aces in a pack, you can perform the astonishing stunt of always cutting an ace.

THE DOTTED CARD is marked with two pencil marks on its back: one at the upper left and the other at the lower right corner. A slight fanning of the cards to the right will permit you quickly to locate this card.

THE BROKEN CARD is easily prepared by breaking three-sixteenth-inch triangles at the upper left and lower right corners. Don't break these corners off; just fracture them, so to speak. Riffle the pack at either of these corners and you will find that the broken card behaves exactly like a short card, falling with a snap and a break in rhythm.

THE NICKED CARD, like the broken-corner card, may be prepared during a performance. Simply press your thumbnail or fingernail straight into the edge of a card, making a tiny nick in it. This way you can transform a borrowed pack into a key-card pack in about one second. The nicked edge is readily cut to, if you know where to look for it.

The Pre-Arranged Deck

There are numerous pre-arranged decks and one is about as good as another. The principle employed is to work out a sequence which appears haphazard but in which every card is—to the person in the know—a key to the card which follows it. The Eight Kings deck is described here.

Arrange the cards as follows: 8S, KH, 3D, 10C, 2S, 7H, 9D, 5C, QS, 4H, AD, 6C, JS, 8H, KD, 3C, 10S, 2H, 7D, 9C, 5S, QH, 4D, AC, 6S, JH, 8D, KC, 3S, 10H, 2D, 7C, 9S, 5H, QD, 4C, AS, 6H, JD, 8C, KS, 3H, 10D, 2C, 7S, 9H, 5D, QC, 4S, AH, 6D, JC.

Now, memorize the sentence, "Eight kings threatened to save ninety-five queens for one sick knave."

Every syllable in that sentence, with the exception of the *ed* in *threatened* and the *y* in *ninety,* suggests one of the thirteen cards. *Theatened* equals three, ten; *save* equals seven, and *sick* equals six. So, if you will say that sentence to yourself, you'll be able to determine the numerical value of any card if you know the card above or below it.

Also, the suits run in bridge-value order: spades, hearts, diamonds, clubs.

Suppose you cut the deck. The six of spades is on the face of your cut. By repeating the sentence you know that a jack follows a six. Hearts follow spades. So the next card must be the jack of hearts.

Eights, of course, follow jacks. The deck is a sort of endless circle. It makes no difference how often it is cut; the sequence won't be disturbed. The magical possibilities of this deck are obviously great. By breaking the deck just above the place where a card is withdrawn and placing this upper part of the pack on the bottom, you have your "index" card where you can conveniently glimpse it. Thus, you can quickly determine any card selected.

You can perform an effective mind-reading trick by asking a spectator to remove four or five cards (that are together). Glimpse your index card and you can name all the cards he holds.

Have a spectator fan any deck while you select a card and return it. Then you fan an Eight Kings deck while he selects and returns a card, the identity of which you quickly learn. Tell your helper to pick his card out of his deck, while you pick yours out of your deck. Naturally, you locate his, and the cards turn out to be duplicates.

And you can always conclude a selection of tricks with this deck by performing a staggering feat. You sit down at the table, have the cards cut, and proceed to deal four perfect bridge hands!

Strippers

In a stripper pack, one end of every card is a fraction of an inch wider than the other end. The cards are arranged so that the wide ends are all together. When a card has been selected, the pack is casually reversed before its return. The wide end of the selected card now protrudes slightly at the edges of the deck because it is among the narrow ends of all the other cards. It may be easily cut to by the sense of touch alone.

The stripper pack is probably the most widely known of all trick packs; for many years it has been hawked at carnivals, fairs, and on street corners. But with a little imagination and showmanship, you can even fool people who know its secret. I once saw Cardini do an impromptu routine with a pack of strippers. Unembarrassed, I confess he had me guessing on several counts. (Incidentally, if you have never seen Cardini, catch his act the first chance you get. You will get a demonstration of misdirection and showmanship that you won't forget.)

The first thing to work out is an unnoticeable way of reversing the pack. Here is a good one: Hold the cards in the right hand, fanning them with the left fingers to have one chosen. When the spectator has the card in his fingers, transfer the pack to the left hand, closing the fan and reversing the deck as you do so.

THE HANGMAN. Have the selected card returned to a reversed pack of strippers. Shuffle the cards, taking care not to reverse any of them. Fan the cards to show that the chosen one is not near the top or bottom. Hold the pack by its edges near the end where the card projects. Hold it in the right hand, in a vertical position, face of the deck toward the audience. Rest the bottom end of the deck on the back of the left hand. Say that the cards are fifty-two murder suspects and your hands are a gallows. Tell the spectator who chose the card, "The guilty suspect is known only to you. You must tell me if I hang the right man." Suddenly drop your left hand, springing the trap. Fifty-one cards fall to the floor. The selected one remains in your right fingers.

One-Way Backs

Many decks have a back design that is not symmetrical. Arrange such a deck so that the designs all point the same way. Reverse the deck after a card has been selected and before it is returned. You can then easily locate this card by its reversed pattern.

For conjuring purposes, it is recommended that you use cards whose one-way nature is not so obvious as that of many of the bridge decks that are so common. The Bicycle "League" deck is an excellent one.

THE TELL-TALE THOUGHT. Have a card selected and returned, reversed, to a one-way deck. Place the deck on the table and ask the spectator to cut and then deal the cards, glancing at the face of each. He is not to stop when he reaches his card or make any motion that might be a give-away. Of course, you are able to recognize the chosen card by its reversed back design. As soon as the dealer has this card in his hand, stop him. Say that you notice a jiggle in his thought waves, and opine that he is now holding his card!

The Svengali Deck

Like the stripper deck, the Svengali deck has become a well-known novelty. It is primarily a forcing deck—it will always force the same card. It consists of twenty-six *short* cards which are identical in suit and rank, and twenty-six *regular* cards of different values. The short and regular cards alternate throughout the deck. When you riffle the cards at either end, the short cards fall concealed behind the regular ones. As a result, the pack appears to be an ordinary one of different cards. But wherever a spectator reaches into the riffled pack to remove a card, there will always be one of the twenty-six identical short cards under his finger!

You can dovetail shuffle a Svengali deck without impairing its function, as long as you shuffle by riffling at the ends of the cards. This advantage, incidentally, is not usually mentioned in the instructions that come with the deck—an oversight which provides you with a clue for confusing the casual buyer, who seldom realizes that so intricate a deck can be shuffled.

Chapter 8

Sudden Stuff

"It is not strength, but art obtains the prize."

ALEXANDER POPE

PROBABLY YOU have noticed that most card tricks fit a formula: A card is selected. Though its identity is hidden from the performer, he reveals it in a magical manner.

There is endless variation, of course, in the way the card is revealed. Let's suppose you are doing card tricks at a party. You might begin with a trick where you simply name a selected card, pretending to read a spectator's mind. You could follow this with the Card on the Wall, the Do as I Do trick, the Spelling Trick, and finally the Telephone Trick. You have not deviated from the formula, yet you have presented an entertaining and varied program.

Still, you will improve the flavor of your program if you will salt it with tricks that follow a different pattern—brief mirages where cards vanish, jump around, change their spots. This branch of magic is called "manipulative" card magic, but don't let that scare you. In many ways it is the most interesting kind of conjuring, to both performer and spectators. The tricks are very simple. They are startling and perplexing to watch; and they will expand your reputation for slickness. You will find yourself the target of such semi-complimentary remarks as, "I'd hate to play poker with you!" And the little-number-with-the-big-eyes will tell you that you are *clever,* in a tone that suggests cleverness is synonymous with sex-appeal.

None of these tricks requires hours of grueling practice.

All demand a certain amount of patience in working out a precise and graceful handling of the cards—just enough digital exercise to be good for your arthritis. The best misdirection for covering this "sudden stuff"—in addition to the misdirection innate in each sleight—is to present four or five of the tricks in a rapid-fire routine. Before the spectator has time to think about one effect, bang! confront him with another.

Let's begin with some *color changes*.

The Thumb-Steal Color Change

EFFECT: The slickster shows the bottom card of the deck. He passes his right hand over its face, transforming it to another card. The spectators think he has simply palmed the bottom card. But he shows his right hand empty.

METHOD: Hold the deck in the left hand with the bottom card exposed. Edges are parallel to the floor. The left thumb is on the upper edge, fingers on the lower. The right hand takes the deck so that its end goes into the crotch of

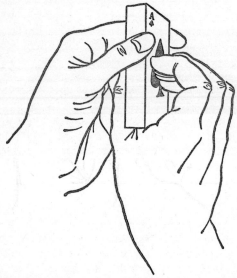

The Thumb-Steal Color Change—Taking the Deck into Right Hand

the little finger at the opposite corner. The right fingers bend inward until their tips are in a straight line across the center of the bottom card. The ball of the right thumb presses against the back of the top card.

Call attention to the suit and value of the bottom card (half of which is exposed above the tips of the bent right fingers). Transfer the deck back to its original position in the left hand, but withdraw the right hand in this manner: Straighten the fingers, keeping their tips against the face of the bottom card at its center. At the same time, draw the top card of the deck into the right palm with the right thumb. Draw the right fingers toward the end of the deck until the top card is clear and snaps into the palm.

Push the right fingers forward in a light rubbing motion, sliding the palmed card between them and the bottom card. The left forefinger should be at the far end of the deck to insure a square fit. The bottom card appears to have been changed like a chameleon by that brief rub of your hand.

When you have completed the change, withdraw your

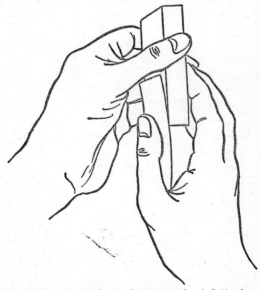

Stealing Top Card as Deck is Returned to Left Hand

right hand in a rigid, unnatural position. Keep its back toward the spectators as if you were awkwardly palming a card. They think you caused the change by lifting off the bottom card. Give them a moment to get good and suspicious; then slowly show your right hand empty.

The Slip-Slide Color Change

This color change is perhaps the neatest and most astonishing of them all. Hold the deck in the left hand between the top joint of the thumb at the center of one edge and the tips of the last three fingers on the opposite edge. The first finger is at the end. The edges of the cards parallel the floor. The bottom card is exposed.

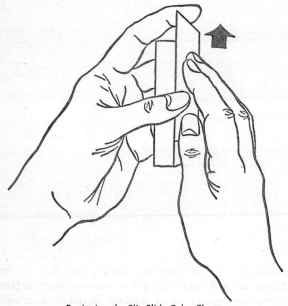

Beginning the Slip-Slide Color Change

Cover the bottom card with the right hand. Secretly slide this card half an inch over the far end of the deck. Move the left forefinger to the end of this protruding card. A half-inch section of the card next to the bottom may now be caught by the right palm below the bases of the fingers.

Slide back the right hand to expose most of the bottom card again, as if you are making sure that the audience sees what this card is. Under cover of your right hand, you secretly draw back the card next to the bottom until the ends of the two cards are clear of each other. Now shove the right hand forward again, slipping the next-to-the-bottom card onto the bottom. The left forefinger, under

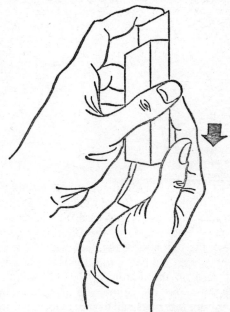

Stealing the Card above the Bottom Card

cover of the right fingers, squares its end of the deck. Spreading your right hand as you pull it back to reveal the change will give the audience the illusion that they see the card change color through the spaces between your fingers.

As the name suggests, color changes should be done with the cards arranged to change a red card to a black one or vice versa.

The Double Color Change

EFFECT: Half the deck is pushed forward to expose part of the face of a card in the center, as well as the face of the bottom card. The magician causes both cards to change color.

Ready for the Double Color Change

METHOD: Hold the cards as for previous changes. Slide the bottom half of the deck forward about an inch over the first finger. Try to have a red card on the face of each packet and a black card on the back of each packet. Thumb-steal the top card of the deck with the right hand. Cover the two exposed cards with this hand and leave the concealed card on the bottom of the deck. At the same time, push downward on the top card of the bottom packet with the left forefinger (its nail engages the end of the card) until this card squarely covers the face of the upper packet. Withdraw your right hand to reveal that the cards on the faces of both parts of the deck have changed.

Other good color changes may be performed by palming a card off the deck by any of the methods given in Chapter 3.

Now let's learn some *switches*—methods of exchanging one single card for another. These are often used as means of revealing selected cards: the performer produces the wrong card, rubs it on his trouser leg, and shows that it has changed to the right one. You see how tough it is to get away from the formula. But switches are also effective in a routine of "sudden stuff," where the magician changes a card he picks at random.

The Double Card

Show the top two cards as one, lifting them between the right thumb at one end and forefinger at the other. Return them to the top. Pause a moment without removing the right hand from the deck. Raise the single top card, face toward you, and blow on it. Show that the face of the card has changed.

This may sound childishly simple, but with misdirection and nerve it can be made very deceptive. I have used it for many years.

A Top Change

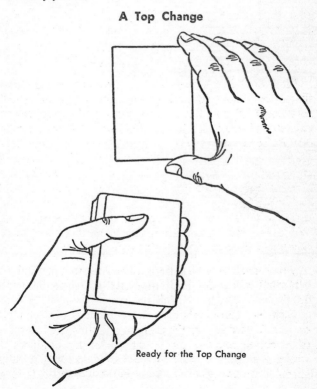

Ready for the Top Change

You can do this change the first time you try, but you should practice it until you develop confidence and smoothness before you exhibit it. To perform any sleight hesitantly is to expose it.

Hold the deck in your left hand in position for dealing. Lift the top card with the right thumb on the lower right corner and the right forefinger on the upper right corner. Show the face of the card. As you do this, push the card that is now on top of the deck a quarter of an inch to the right with the left thumb. Return the card in your right hand to the top of the deck, gripping the card below it between the right thumb and second finger tip the instant

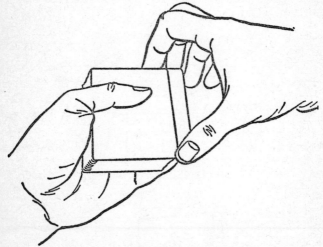

Changing Card in Right Hand for Top Card

they touch it. Without the slightest pause, lift the deck away with the left hand, raising it to show the bottom card. Do not move the right hand. Make some remark about the bottom card, then show that the one in your right hand has changed.

The One-Hand Change

Show the two top cards as one, holding them in your right hand with their lower end in the crotch of the thumb.

The right fingers are bent so that their tips are across the center of this double card on its back. The ball of the right thumb is in the center of its face. Show the face of the card. Turn the back of the card toward the spectators. Appear to place this card on the table, but really shove the upper card forward with your fingers and leave it instead. The hand at

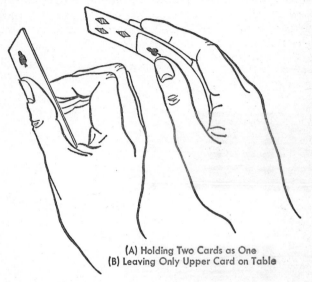

(A) Holding Two Cards as One
(B) Leaving Only Upper Card on Table

once returns to the deck and quietly drops its burden there. Reveal the change by asking a bystander to turn up the card on the table.

The Downs Change

Hold the deck in the crotch of your left thumb in position for dealing but with the faces of the cards up. Lift the bottom two cards as one and move them about an inch to the right. The left thumb holds them in place by pressing against the center of the face of the bottom card. The four left finger tips press against the back of the next-to-the-bottom card where it protrudes over the edge of the deck.

The right fingers approach to take this card. As they do so, the left hand revolves toward the body, turning the deck over. During this turning motion, the left thumb pulls the bottom card back even with the rest of the deck; and the right hand takes only the next-to-the-bottom card.

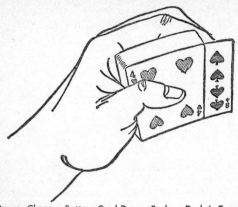

The Downs Change. Bottom Card Drawn Back as Deck Is Turned Over

Rub this card on your trouser leg (or your nylons) and then reveal the change.

The Glide

Hold the deck in the left hand, face up, between the thumb on one edge and the first three fingers on the other. The first finger should be down about an inch from its end of the deck. The cards slant from this end toward the palm, so that the whole top joint of the third finger may be bent over the face of the bottom card at the lower right corner.

Show the bottom card to the spectators. Turn the deck over, bringing the backs of the cards upward. Hold the deck parallel to the table top. You'll find it an easy matter to draw back the bottom card with the third finger. Your right fingers now go to the bottom of the deck and appear to take the bottom card; in reality, they draw off the next-to-the-bottom card.

Here is an excellent trick utilizing the glide:

The Fading Pips

Place the three of hearts on the bottom of the deck with the ace of hearts immediately above it. Cover each of the two end pips of this bottom card with a thumb, so that

The Glide. Bottom Card Is Drawn Back with Third Finger

only the middle pip is visible. Announce that the ace of hearts is on the bottom. The spectators will see the indices or realize from the awkward position of your hands that you are trying to pass the three as the ace. Turn the pack over, performing the glide and laying the real ace of hearts on the table.

Pretend to overhear one of the audience make an uncomplimentary remark regarding your skill as a prestidigitator. Of course, you may not have to pretend. Look hurt. Ask this spectator to turn over the card.

Another way to present the trick is to offer to bet one of

the spectators that he can't name the card on the table. He'll think he has you and will name the three of hearts. He turns over the ace. This is an especially good way to nonplus the guy who thinks he knows all about cards because he played poker once for fifty-cent chips and who has been trying to cross you up all evening.

Production of a Fan of Cards

Hold the deck in the color-change position. Cover its face for a second with the right fingers, thumb at rear. With the left first finger push about a third of the cards off the top into the crotch of the right thumb. Without hesitation,

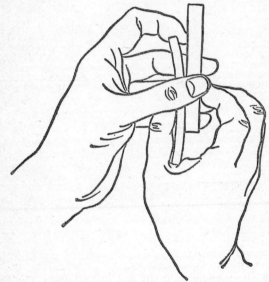

Production of a Fan—Stealing the Cards

raise the right hand to the left elbow, briefly touch your sleeve as if drawing it up (this is important!), then move the hand under and to the rear of the elbow. Bend your two middle fingers over the ends of the cards, clipping them against your palm until the thumb can move to a position against the face of the bottom card. Holding the cards between the thumb and fingers, move the thumb toward your left hand and the fingers toward your left shoulder, fanning the cards. Reveal this fan just below the left elbow, as if you picked it out of the air.

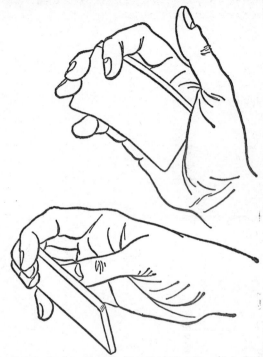

Production of a Fan—Showing How Cards Are Moved into Position for Fanning

Return these cards to the bottom of the deck, but hold a break above them with the left little finger. Square the deck with the right hand, palm the cards below the break, and produce them in another fan—this time from behind the left knee.

Vanish of the Deck

EFFECT: The trickster produces a fan of cards from under his elbow. He remarks that he now has a deck in each hand (of course he actually has only two *half* decks) but that he has no need for two decks. He makes a fanning motion near the cards in his left hand with the cards in his right. The left-hand "deck" disappears.

METHOD: Produce the fan. Keeping your right side turned toward the audience, cover the squared-up cards in the left hand with the fan. Clip them between the right third and fourth fingers, holding them concealed behind the fan. Turn the left hand so that its back is toward the audience; keep the left fingers bent as if they still hold their cards. The instant the left hand is turned over, lower the fan a few inches in the beginning of the fanning motion. Continue this two or three times below the left hand. Finally, with a tossing motion, show the left hand empty.

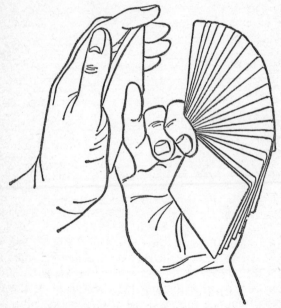

Vanish of the Deck—Stealing the Cards

Two points should be emphasized: (1) The left-hand packet is covered by the fanned cards for only a fraction of a second. (2) The tossing motion is made leisurely and gracefully as if the cards suddenly turned to vapor, which you are scattering into the atmosphere. If that sounds senseless, the next time you see a professional magician, watch the way he opens his hand when he shows that some object has vanished from it. You will see that there is an artistic way of doing this that gives the spectators the impression that they see the object fade away. Try this: Close your left hand into a fist. Imagine that you have a card crumpled up in it. First, snap your fingers open to show that the card has vanished. Now, close your hand again. This time open it slowly and gracefully as if the card has turned into a puff of smoke that is going to float out of your palm. Do you see what I mean?

A Routine of Quick Changes

As an example of the sort of fast and flashy routine that can be worked up from the material in this chapter, I have outlined the following combination of sleights. I offer it merely as a pattern on which you can base routines of your own which include the sleights you like best.

Show the top card, holding it in position for the top change. Let's suppose this card is the four of spades. Do the top change and show the bottom card, which we'll suppose is the three of hearts. Say, "I'll put the four of spades on the bottom." Put the indifferent card you hold in your hand on the bottom, as if it were the four of spades. Snap the deck and show that the four of spades has jumped to the top. Say, "Now I'll put it second from the top." Do so, but hold a break under the top cards with the little finger tip. Snap the deck again and lift the two top cards, showing them as one. Return the double card to the top. Lift off the top single card as if it were the four and shove it into the center of the deck. Show that the four has jumped to the top again. Show the bottom card, which is the indifferent one you put there a while back, and say, "I wonder what happened to the three of hearts?" Appear to shift the bottom card to the top; but do the glide, really putting the three of hearts on top. Again snap the pack; quickly show the two top cards as one—the four of spades.

Say you'll put it on the bottom but really put the three of hearts there. Show that the four is again on top—and the three on the bottom.

See how you can work out a fast series of astonishing effects? You can work in a color change or two, if you like. Or, cut the pack, performing the slip, and show that the four of spades jumps to the top again. Perform a routine of this sort boldly and without hesitation. Don't give the spectator time to think.

The next trick perhaps doesn't belong in this chapter, because it reverts to the formula we have been trying to avoid. On the other hand, it is a quick change.

The Fickle Heart

EFFECT: A card is selected and shuffled into the deck by a spectator. The magician puts the deck into its case. He tells the spectator to think hard of his card in an effort to think it to the bottom of the deck. When the bottom card is shown, however, it proves to be the wrong one. It is the right suit, but has one spot too many. Unabashed, the magician snaps off the extra pip.

METHOD: Cut a heart pip from an old card. Remove the five of hearts from the pack you are going to use, and with an eraser rub off the pip in the center of the card. It can be neatly and completely erased. With a bit of beeswax, or the tiniest dab of chewing gum, stick the cut-out pip on the blank center of the five. Leave this card in the card-case while you do your preliminary tricks.

Force the four of hearts. Let the spectator shuffle; then put the cards into their case (on top of the prepared card). Mention incidentally that you are doing this to preclude the possibility of manipulation of the cards. Talk about the power of the mind to influence the positions of the cards. Carefully remove the deck from the case. Show the five of hearts as if the trick had been brought to its conclusion. When the spectator tells you that his card was the *four* of hearts, act as if you think he must be mistaken. Finally say, "Well, I missed by only one pip. Hearts are fickle cards, anyway—easily changed." Holding the deck by its ends in the left hand, bend it backward slightly to make the edges of the pip stand out. Snap it off with the right forefinger.

You'll find that half the time the audience doesn't even see the loose pip sail through the air—you seem to make it disappear entirely!

Chapter 9

Gamblers' Sleights

"So for a good old-gentlemanly vice
I think I must take up avarice."

GEORGE GORDON, LORD BYRON

MANY PROFESSIONAL MAGICIANS delight in exposing the artifices of the crooked gambler. While such exposés are entertaining, they usually contain a lot of misinformation and I doubt that they accomplish anything beyond establishing in the wide-eyed onlookers a false confidence in their ability to detect crooked dealing. The magicians rather sanctimoniously emphasize their own use of trickery as a means of entertainment and vehemently condemn those who use it as a means of defrauding the public. Secretly, I sometimes suspect that their bitterness is of a personal nature. I wonder if at some time in his life the exposer wasn't thoroughly fleeced. For when it comes to perfection of physical skill and mastery of their own peculiar misdirection, the gamblers generally make the professional magicians look like a bunch of kids playing games with box tops.

Let me tell you about a bottom-dealer I knew in the Army. He used to practice hours at a time, dealing alternate cards from the top and bottom of the deck. There was only one way that I could tell which cards came off the bottom. That was to lie on the floor and see the change on the face of the deck. Once, I mentioned that I had heard of people who could detect bottom-dealing by ear. That worried him. He thought he could distinguish a slight difference in sound between his own tops and bottoms. Now, that guy cherished his sleep as much as any soldier, but he sat up all night, practicing until he had eliminated that difference in sound—which I couldn't notice anyway!

All crooked gamblers aren't like that, of course. I've seen some pretty crude performers. But these lads usually end up with broken heads—after which they get either religion or perfection.

The card sharp usually devotes his life to two or three sleights. They represent his living, his dream, and his social security. He often pairs up with another sharp and they work as a team. They plan a system of signals and devise a strategy that will turn every possible chance in their favor. In addition to being adept cheaters, they are also adroit players; and when the cards are falling favorably they do not resort to subterfuge. That's another reason why it's hard to detect a sharp—at the moment you are watching him he may be dealing as honestly as a parson playing old maid with the children.

Another interesting thing about the crooked dealer: He doesn't generally refer to members of his profession by such terms as *shark, sharp, fast-dealer,* or other glamorous synonyms for *cheater*. He says *cheater,* right out loud!

The picture I am going to give you of the art of the gambler must be framed in one chapter; therefore, it is an abbreviated one. But it will give you at least a nodding acquaintance with a subject your friends are sure to ask about when they recognize your proficiency with the pasteboards.

Do as you like about learning the sleights. Many of them are readily adaptable to conjuring purposes, but whether they are worth the arduous practice necessary for their perfection is up to you. The first time you try second-and bottom-dealing, it may seem impossible to you that these ruses can ever be brought to a point where a sharp eye can't detect them. Let me assure you that they can. There is only one way to detect an accomplished crooked dealer: make sure that the light is exactly right and focus a high-speed movie camera on his hands. The slow-motion pictures will reveal the true actions of his fingers, which the human eye is not fast enough to catch.

The Second-Deal

It is common among crooks to mark the high cards during the first few hands of play. They do this by nicking the edges, secretly applying specks of special ink, smearing the cards with cigarette ashes, scratching the backs with the point of a needle, crimping according to a pattern, or any of a dozen other ways. Sometimes they get a previously marked deck into the game. However the marking is accomplished, it not only furnishes an index to what cards the opponents hold—it also facilitates the dealer's task of providing himself with a good hand.

Suppose that, during the deal, the sharp comes upon a card whose secret mark designates an ace. Instead of dealing that card, he deals the one under it, repeating this action until he can deal the ace to himself or his partner. This is second-dealing. Needless to say, it must be performed so that the top card seems to be dealt.

Hold the deck in your left hand in position for dealing. The left thumb is on the back of the top card near the top end. The left fingers are on the right edge of the deck, their tips even with the top card.

The right hand approaches, thumb and first finger going to the upper right hand corner of the deck. The left thumb pushes this corner of the top card to the right and toward

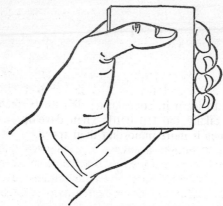

How Deck Is Held for the Second-Deal

your body, exposing the corner of the second card. The right thumb draws off this second card. The instant it is clear, the left thumb snaps the top card flush with the

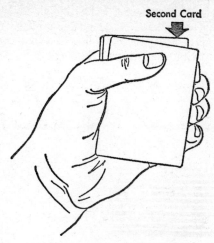

Second Card

The Second Card Exposed for Dealing

others. This action is covered by the left hand's moving to the left with a not-too-noticeable bending of the wrist. As you become proficient, you'll be able to reduce the movement of the left hand to the left.

The whole action is done in a flash and is immediately repeated. As the hands approach each other, the left thumb again pushes the top card to the right. The right fingers appear to take it but really take the second card.

The second-deal described above is usually done fast—at the rate of about three cards dealt per second. But, if you decide to learn it, concentrate first on perfecting the illusion of taking the top card. Then develop a smooth rhythm, which is more important than speed.

Second- and bottom-dealing are usually not done with cards whose backs have a white border. A small monotonous pattern is best. Most card-table pirates prefer Bee cards, back number 67, for this sort of work. Club Reno, number 103, is also an excellent back design.

Another Second-Deal

Deals similar to this one are described in old books on trickery, but they always seemed to me about as practical as a glass hammer. Then a girl dealer in Reno, Nevada, did this one for me. She'd worked the moves out for herself and had it down to the point where she could do it quite slowly without destroying the illusion. Though it may

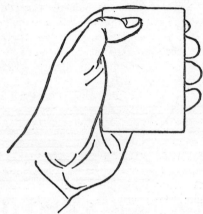

How to Hold Deck for "Another Second-Deal"

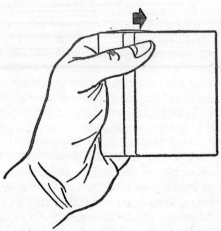

Pushing Second Card to Right under Top Card

seem easier at first, it is much harder to perfect than the other second-deal.

Place the deck on the left fingers. Its left edge should slant from the top of the bump at the base of the first finger to the bottom of the bump at the base of the little finger. The tips of the fingers press the deck against the palm, holding it firm. The thumb is bent to rest on the top card near the left edge.

Push the top card half an inch to the left with the *side* of the left thumb. Turn the thumb so that its ball touches the back of the second card as well as that of the top card. Shove these two cards to the right until the thumb is straight. The left finger tips prevent your shoving over three cards instead of two.

Withdraw the second card with the right fingers underneath it and the right thumb on top. At the same instant, bend the left thumb again to snap the top card flush with the deck. Again shove over two cards in the same manner. And so forth. You will find that the top card has a tendency to swing out at the bottom after several consecutive seconds have been dealt. It is straightened by bumping it with the right little finger as a card is dealt.

The Bottom-Deal

The correct position for bottom-dealing is extremely hard to describe. Hold the deck face toward left palm. Place the tip of the left middle finger against the bottom half of the cards, squarely on the upper right corners of these cards. Push the lower left corner of the deck as high into the palm as you can get it. Now adjust this position so that the upper left corner of the deck fits neatly into the crook of the left forefinger. The two upper joints of this finger should be parallel to and against the ends of the cards; the lower joint is almost parallel to the sides of the cards. This forefinger exerts no pressure and has nothing to do with gripping the deck, which is held only between the tip of the middle finger and the palm.

Make another adjustment: place the tip of the left third finger against the face of the bottom card at its upper index.

Place the left thumb on the back of the top card, its tip pointing at the upper right corner.

If the position feels cramped you probably have it right! You are ready to deal.

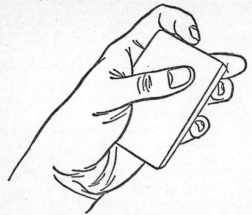

How to Hold Deck for the Bottom-Deal

Push the top card to the right with the left thumb. At the same time, press the third finger against the bottom card near the upper right corner; press toward the palm, forcing this card to buckle downward. Having thus freed it, shove it to the right under the protruding top card.

In the meantime, the right hand has approached the deck. The right forefinger curls over the end of the extended top card. The tip of this finger is low enough to be below the bottom card when the latter is kicked out by the left third finger. The left thumb snaps the top card back to its original position just as the right thumb and finger close. They carry away the bottom card as the left hand withdraws the deck.

Discouraged? The knack is to grip the pack only between the middle finger tip and the palm and to be sure that the lower part of the middle finger is not pressed against the bottom card in such a way as to clamp it in place. You'll know when you have the position just right, because the third finger will be able to buckle back the bottom card and shove it to the right with ease.

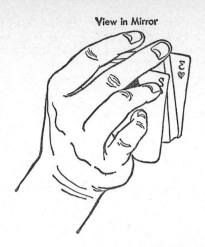

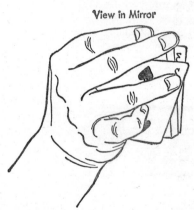

Worm's Eye View of the Bottom-Deal

The illusion of taking the top card is as good as in the second-deal. The right thumb may actually touch this card just before it is snapped out of the way. Some of the nimble-fingered gentry perform the bottom-deal indetectably with *one hand*—a useful feat in stud poker.

I suppose that a perfect bottom-deal has made a lot of unscrupulous characters rich. I dare say that an imperfect one has made a lot more of them hospital patients. Outraged poker players sometimes inflict a particularly nasty, if poetically just, vengeance—broken hands.

Running Up a Hand

The professionl sharp usually culls his hand as he assembles the deck for the shuffle and deal. At a glance, he chooses from the discards and face-up hands (assuming that the game is poker) the cards he wants to deal himself. He easily gets them to the top or bottom. If he is to use the bottom deal, he palms these cards while the pack is cut, returns them to the bottom, and deals. But many gamblers prefer to stack their hand during the shuffle.

Remember the gambler's shuffle? You learned it as a false shuffle that will keep the top half of the deck in order. There are dozens of applications of this shuffle, some very elaborate, which make is possible to stack cards so they will fall to the dealer or to any other player he wishes.

Suppose the dealer has assembled a full house on the bottom of the deck. He holds the cards in position for an overhand shuffle, top of the deck to the left. He undercuts more than half the deck. The left thumb draws the top card of this packet onto the packet in the left hand, but at the same time the left fingers draw a card off the *bottom* of the right-hand packet. The left hand now draws three more cards (one at a time) from the top of the right-hand packet. Then (supposing the game to be a five-handed one) cards are again pulled from the top and bottom simultaneously. This continues until each of the five cards in the full house is stacked with four cards on top of it. The next card is injogged and the gambler's shuffle is continued as you already know it.

Here's another method of running up a hand during an overhand shuffle. The formula may be varied to fit the size of the game and the number of cards to be stacked. We assume that the game is five-handed and that the dealer wants to give himself three aces, which are on top of the pack.

With the deck in the left hand in shuffling position, lift a packet from the *top*—which is to the left—in the right fingers. Shuffle seven cards singly from this packet onto

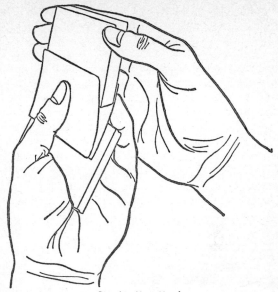

Running Up a Hand

the other. Drop the right-hand packet behind (to the right of) the other. Lift the whole deck with the right fingers and run six cards into the left palm. Return these to the top of the deck. Undercut a packet; shuffle four cards from it onto the left-hand packet, and return the right-hand packet to the bottom of the deck. Shuffle five cards from the top of the deck into the left palm and return them to the top. Undercut a packet and shuffle four cards from it onto the other packet. Injog, and perform the gambler's shuffle as you know it. You have stacked yourself the three aces below the injog.

This method of running up a hand makes a mystifying trick, if you work out a shuffle that looks natural. Don't snap the cards or otherwise give the impression you are counting.

The Cut

How about the cut? How does the gambler beat that little custom?

The truth is that the cut is a thorn in the gambler's side and a pain in his neck. Through the ages, he has developed many schemes to nullify the cut. The regular pass was indubitably devised for this purpose, and it is still used. It can, with a minimum of misdirection, be performed indectably at the card table (see Covering the Pass, Chapter 3).

The use of the bridge is common. The gambler cuts the cards himself, bridging the top portion, before he invites his neighbor to cut. The chances are good that the latter will cut at the bridge.

Of course, if two sharps are working together, the cut need be a problem for only one of them. And many poker players are superstitious about cutting. "Cut dog never has pups," they recite, and they wave the deck away. If he can arrange it, the gambler sits to the left of one of these charitable characters.

The bottom-dealer, since he has only three or four cards whose position he wants to preserve, usually palms them when he offers the deck for the cut and replaces them after the cut is made. This maneuver is a difficult one to perfect. Here is an excellent way to accomplish it, if you are interested:

Hold the deck in the left hand in the crotch of the thumb. The thumb extends across the *lower* end of the deck, its tip touching the tip of the first finger, which is against the right edge at the corner. The right hand now grips the deck with the thumb at the inner end and first and second finger tips at the outer end near the right corner. At the lower right corner, the left second finger breaks away the packet of cards to be palmed, pushing them toward the left palm. This forces the upper right corner of the packet to protrude slightly. The right third finger presses against this corner at the front end, pivoting these bottom cards against the base of the left thumb at their lower left corner until they swing neatly into the left palm. The left hand turns toward the body as the right presents the deck for the cut.

If you'll try this a few times, you'll see that endless practice is necessary to bring this palm to the point where it can

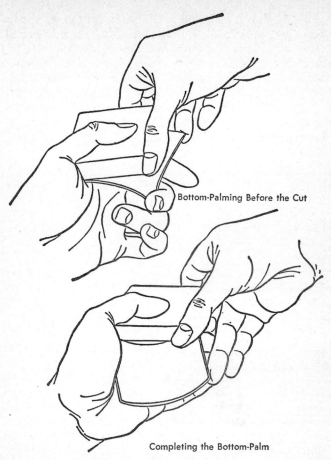

Bottom-Palming Before the Cut

Completing the Bottom-Palm

be performed under the eagle eyes of habitual poker players. And you'll realize that something more than practice is needed—nerve. The time taken by the cut must seem an eternity to the man with the damning evidence in his left palm.

The gambler has devised scores of *slips* or *shifts* to reverse the halves of the deck after the cut has been made. I have no intention of including any of these here, because none is better than the regular pass and many aren't so good. In poker, the bottom-dealer sometimes deals the first hands without making the pass—but holding the break. When he has dealt himself his last card, he makes the pass as he transfers the deck to his right hand and places it on the table. He waits until this moment because it is one when the other players are picking up their hands and, each according to his own luck-making ritual, looking at their cards. He then deals himself his bottoms on the draw.

The usual method of slipping the cut which the magicians demonstrate in their exposés is one which is seldom, if ever, used in play. It makes quite an impression on an audience, however; so I'll explain it.

Pick up the bottom portion of the deck with the right thumb on its left edge, forefinger on the back of the top card and second finger on the face of the bottom card. Once the packet is off the table, the thumb plays no part in holding it; it is gripped between the first two fingers only. Its lower right corner should rest against the base of the little finger.

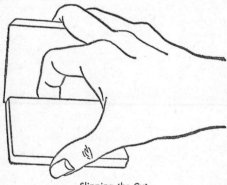

Slipping the Cut

This bottom packet is moved to a position directly over the one on the table. It is then revolved to the left and its left edge placed against the table top to the right of the packet on the table. The thumb and forefinger then pick up the top packet. The forefinger is withdrawn and the deck snaps together in its original order.

128

To Glimpse the Bottom Card: Hold the deck in your left hand in position for dealing. Grip it with the right hand, fingers at front end, thumb at rear. The right thumb should extend well below the bottom card. Shove the deck forward one inch, pressing it downward so that the bottom card is held against the left first and buckles against the right thumb. Push until you get a glimpse of the index.

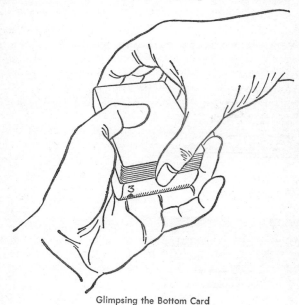

Glimpsing the Bottom Card

This is also a good way to put a crimp across one end of a card.

To Glimpse the Top Card at Stud Poker: Suppose you have dealt the first two rounds of a five-card stud game. Each player has a down-card and an up-card. Raise the lower left corner of the top card with your right thumb. Catch the left edge of this card against the fleshy part of the left thumb, so that the corner remains raised a quarter of an inch. As you peek at your hole-card, raising its inner end with the right fingers, hold it down with the knuckles of the left hand. This natural action points the inner end of the pack at your eyes and allows you to glimpse the index of the top card—and of the bottom card as well.

DEALING EXTRAS. Another petty ruse is to deal oneself too many cards. The chiseler then either discards too many, or he palms the extra cards and drops them on top of the pack. The latter course has the additional advantage of letting the dealer know the first cards of the draw.

THE TWIST. I am tempted to put the description of this move in capital letters, because it has cost a lot of suckers a lot of money. It requires nerve rather than digital skill. For that reason it is one of the commonest of all methods of cheating, having been used—I am told—even in really big games where the players were supposed to be hard to cheat. It is now so well known among gamblers that I suppose it will soon be useless. But I have never seen it described in print before.

It is performed at that propitious moment when the players pick up their hands.

The dealer has the hand he wants on the bottom. He has dealt with it there, holding a break above it with a finger tip or with the fleshy part of his thumb. He has dealt his own hand into a neat packet in front of him. He now picks up this packet with the forefinger at one end and thumb at the other. He boldly lays these cards on top of the deck, and with his right hand lifts off that part of the deck above the break. As the right hand moves away, placing the deck on the table, the left hand fans the cards it holds. You have to try this to see how deceptive it is.

Cheating at Bridge

If I were to make my living as a parasite of the pasteboards, I'd brush up on Culbertson, get myself an unscrupulous partner, and find some nice people who like to play bridge for money. I would pick bridge players to victimize because they are infinitely less wary than other gamblers.

As you doubtless know, most bridge players are strict, not to say fussy, about procedure. They are particularly strict, not to say fussy, about seeing that while one player deals, his partner shuffles another deck for the next deal. Thus, South shuffles a deck which is going to be dealt by East. East offers it to North (the shuffler's partner!) to be cut. If East first shuffles, he is apt to get his head bitten off, or at best to be thought cautious to the point of rudeness. Now, strictness is a fine thing in a card game, but in this case it is making law out of an illogical custom. For there is nothing, short of paralysis, to keep a dishonest partnership from running up a hand and cutting it to the top. The shuffler has all the time in the world. And if there is anyone at the table who is not gabbing his head off and who feels like watching something, the chances are he is watching the deal and not the shuffle. Most important, the shuffler knows that his partner will cut the cards.

Let's be specific.

If you are a bridge player, you will see at once what a terrific advantage one partnership will have if, on every other deal, one partner is sure to hold three high honors in addition to what cards chance brings him. You will also see the added advantage of the other partner's knowing what these honors are.

Suppose you are South in a bridge game. Suppose also that your wife has left you, you're broke, and your faithful dog has been poisoned by your opponents, who are Nazis. After a battle with your conscience, you have decided to cheat.

Riffle the end of the deck until you see an ace or a king you would like to give your partner. Cut this card to the bottom of the right-hand packet, preparatory to a dovetail shuffle. Begin by riffling four cards from the left-hand packet, pop in the honor card next, and finish any old way. Cut again, making another honor the bottom of the right-hand packet. This time drop one card from the left hand packet, then the honor, then let four or more cards fall in a bunch from the left-hand packet before you get careless. Cut a third honor, but to the top of the left-hand packet. Start by riffling at least six cards from the bottom of this packet. Let the cards dovetail at random from then on until you get near the top; then make sure that the top card of the left-hand packet falls under the top two cards of the right-hand packet. In three shuffles, you have culled three cards and stacked them for your partner.

Cut the deck, bridging it slightly above the card you want on top. Place it at East's elbow. When it's his deal he will present it to your partner for the cut. That worthy, as the bridge writers would call him, has been properly prompted to be sure that he cuts at the break.

This system of cheating is based on the procedure of "making" the cards which now seems to be accepted, often insisted on, all over the country. It should be emphasized that the two-deck plan speeds up the game and is essentially a good one. *Properly* observed, it makes cheating difficult. *The dealer should give the cards one shuffle* before presenting them to be cut. This is perfectly proper—see Culbertson's *Gold Book*. I could never understand why so many players disapprove of this shuffle. The practice of omitting it makes bridge a soft touch for the swindler.

You have been initiated into the commonest methods of card-sharping. They make excellent entertainment, either when adapted to tricks or when demonstrated to your friends as accompaniment to a lecture on not playing cards with strangers. If you are interested in delving deeper into the subject, visit a magic shop and ask for a copy of *The Expert at the Card Table* by S. W. Erdnase. Though it was first published in 1902, this "gamblers' Bible" is still the best work on the methods of the cheat.

Chapter 10

Subtle Stuff

"Anything that deceives may be said to enchant."

PLATO

PERHAPS WHEN YOU FIRST picked up this book you thought that the way to become a card wizard was to learn a lot of tricks. I tried to talk you out of that one in a hurry. I hope that by this time you agree that the quick and easy way to learn card magic is to learn technique. If you know how to palm, how to get a card to the top, false shuffle, and force a card—and if you have also developed a sense of misdirection and showmanship, you are far ahead of where you would be if you had merely studied a collection of tricks.

Of course, tricks are important, too. Your knowledge of technique would be wasted unless you had some tricks to apply it to—good tricks. And you know by this time that when I say good tricks I mean good *effects*. Anyway, as you learned technique you also learned some of the best tricks there are in the field of informal conjuring. I have included a large enough number of tricks to allow you to pick and choose—you have a wide range of choice, as the department store people say. Half a dozen tricks, mastered, will win you a reputation as an expert. So choose carefully. Choose the tricks you like best—the ones that seem to fit your own personality. If a trick doesn't seem to be your style, skip it. You don't see Humphrey Bogart playing Little Lord Fauntleroy.

While this book is addressed to the beginner, it provides

—here and there—material that will be of interest to the veteran trickster. If you are a veteran trickster and you haven't already found a trick, a twist, a suggestion, that you can make use of, cheer up. You may find it in this chapter. If you are a novice and have a friend who knows something about card magic, in this chapter lies the principle that will fool him. Most of the tricks that follow (while not all are new) have been adapted to a system of arranging a sequence of cards right under the noses of the spectators. There is no telling how many other strained brains have devised similar systems. But I worked out this very simple one all by myself and I hereby modestly entitle it "The Ne Plus Ultra Whiz-ding Flapjack-Turner Stacking System Par Excellence."

It may be that my mother was frightened by a trick done with stacked cards (late in the summer of 1860), and my prejudice against this type of deception may be otherwise groundless. But, aside from the inconvenience of having to carry your own pack, which is not a comfortable thing to sit on, stacked tricks have always seemed to me less magical than those done on the spur of the moment with borrowed cards. Many experts give me an argument on this point, and my own contention that only the effect of a trick counts may seem to refute it. Anyway, the system that follows makes possible the arranging of a deck during a performance and brings into the impromptu category a feast of tricks that otherwise would require preparation in the privacy of your own kitchen, so to speak. It is based upon

The Set-Up Location

This is a simple location which gives you a chance to pick out the cards you need for your next trick and to stack them. You should give a little extra attention to this trick, building it into an astonishing mystery in itself. This isn't hard. If you appear to be making a real effort to read the spectator's mind, you create a certain amount of suspense as you pick up the cards. As you approach the conclusion and there are fewer and fewer cards left on the table, the suspense grows. The trick is rather long but it is one that will hold attention.

EFFECT: A spectator shuffles. He selects a card and returns it. All the cards are dealt onto the table, faces up. The magician undertakes to read the spectator's mind by applying a process of elimination to the cards. He picks them up a few at a time until only the selected one remains.

METHOD: When a spectator has shuffled to his heart's content, take the pack from him and secretly nick the lower left hand corner of the top card with your right thumbnail. A nick of pin-point size is all that is necessary. Get this marked card to the center of the deck. Keep track of it by holding a break under it. Have a card selected. Make sure that it is returned immediately below the nicked card. Watch for the nick when you deal out the deck. The following card, of course, will be the chosen one. Note it, but go right on dealing. As you near the end of the deal, speed up the process by laying down the cards in bunches.

Pick up a few cards at a time, *stacking whatever sequence you need for the next trick*. If the stack is a perceptible one—for instance, the thirteen hearts in order—pick up the last two or three cards of the sequence first; then two or three indifferent cards, which you put *below* the others. Put another few cards in order on top of those in your hand, a few more indifferent ones on the bottom, etc. It isn't recommended that you stack a complete deck during this trick, but you can arrange up to twenty-six cards without too much trouble.

The mind-reading feat seems to occupy your whole attention. The audience attributes any hesitation on your part to difficulty with this trick. You seem to be bringing about one climax—how can the audience suspect that you are thinking ahead to another?

When you have the necessary cards in order, pick up the bulk of the remaining ones rapidly. Leave the chosen card and two others, which are close to it in suit and number, until last. Mull over these a moment as if genuinely unsure of yourself. Touch the chosen card as if to eliminate it. Hesitate, change your mind, and pick up the other two.

Let's look at a few tricks with which you can follow the set-up location.

Poker Deal

This is the most mystifying dealing trick for entertainment purposes that I know. As you perform the set-up location, you pick up four indifferent cards, a royal heart, four more indifferent cards, another royal heart, etc., continuing until you have stacked yourself a royal flush. False shuffle, false cut, and deal five hands of poker. You can elaborate by stacking the deal given at the end of Chapter 4.

The Think-a-Card Speller

EFFECT: A spectator makes a *mental* selection from a hand of six cards dealt by the trickster. These cards are returned to the pack. The spectator takes the deck into his own hands and spells the name of his card, dealing one card for each letter. He turns over the last card—it is the one he thought of!

METHOD: Remember the spelling trick (Chapter 5)? You learned then that all cards spell in from ten to fifteen letters. By changing the way you spelled, you were always able to spell the twelfth card. Well, in this trick, you stack in order six cards that spell in ten, eleven, twelve, thirteen, fourteen, and fifteen letters. An example would be: ace of clubs, ten of spades, jack of spades, queen of hearts, five of diamonds, and eight of diamonds. Stack them with the ace of clubs on top of the deck, eight of diamonds sixth from the top.

Casually false shuffle. Deal the top six cards. Spread them into a face-up fan on the table, keeping them in order. Ask a spectator to think of one card. Say, "Instead of having you draw a card in the usual way, I wish you would merely think of one of those on the table, etc." When you speak of drawing a card, idly spread the pack to illustrate. Secretly count nine cards (count by three's) from the top and hold a little-finger break under them. Return the fanned cards under these nine. This is a good place for a false cut. Whatever selection the spectator made will always turn up on the last letter of its name.

Perfect Control

EFFECT: A spectator cuts the deck into two halves. From one of these he selects a card and returns it. He names a number between one and ten and counts to that number in the other packet, turning the card that lies there. He notes the number of spots on this card and counts down that number of cards in the first packet. The card at this number proves to be the one he selected.

METHOD: During the set-up location, stack the top ten cards as follows (x indicates an indifferent card): x, 10, x, 10, x, 10, x, 10, x, 9. Suits don't matter.

False shuffle. Invite someone to cut the deck into halves. Have a card selected from that part of the deck that is not stacked, spreading the cards from the left hand into the right. As you do this, count nine cards. Hold a break and have the selected card returned tenth. False shuffle this packet and drop it to the table.

Your assistant names a number from one to ten. If it is an odd number, tell him to count to it and turn the *next* card. If it is an even number, have him turn the card right at that number. Whatever number he names will bring him a ten-spot or, if he names nine or ten, a nine-spot. So he is sure to count to his card in the other packet.

Super Perception

EFFECT: A spectator deals two packets onto the table. He fans one of these without letting the magician see the faces of the cards. He thinks of a number and remembers the card at this number. The cards are in his own hands and the selection is entirely a mental one—he needn't touch the card.

He now mixes the packet to his heart's content to make sure that his card no longer lies at the same number. The mixed cards are returned to the deck. Upon being told the number at which the selected card originally lay, the magician quickly finds it.

METHOD: Stack the top twenty cards by picking up any ten pairs in any order, but don't duplicate any of the pairs. You might begin with a pair of queens, a pair of fives, a pair of aces, etc.

False shuffle. Invite a spectator to deal two packets of ten cards each. Dealing alternately, he will unknowingly deal two packets in which the cards run in the same order. He takes either, fans it, thinks of a number, and remembers the card at that number. Be sure he counts from his left.

In the meantime, you set the deck on the undisturbed packet, pick it up, and note the bottom card (it will be one of the first pair you stacked). When the spectator has shuffled his packet, have him put it on top of the deck. Cut. Apparently, his telling you the number at which his selected card lay, can be of no possible help to you. However, fan the deck and locate the card you noted. The ten cards above this one are numerical duplicates of the ones from which the selection was made and are in the original order. Note the cards at the spectator's number (from the top) in this group of cards. Then find a card of equal value in the mixed-up group—which is the ten cards *below* the card you noted.

Suppose the spectator's number is seven. Suppose the bottom card of the unused packet is the queen of spades. Locate this key card. Starting with it, count ten cards toward the top of the deck. Now find the seventh card down in this group. Let's say it's a four-spot. Look in the ten cards below the queen of spades for another four-spot, which will be the mentally selected card.

Divination Supreme

EFFECT: This trick lives up to its pretentious title. The magician shuffles a pack, drops it on the table, and says he will not touch the cards while a selection is made. The spectator is to deal from the top, stopping whenever he likes. He notes a card at the place where he stopped. He shuffles this card into the deck.

The magician says, "Since I haven't touched the pack, I couldn't possibly know where your card is or what it is. Still you might think that I noted a spot on the back of your card; or perhaps you think I'm sharp-eyed enough to follow your card through its course in a shuffle. So, to make conditions even more difficult—not to say impossible—I am going to ask our host to hand me a new deck which I have never seen before." The magician quickly picks the duplicate of the selected card out of the new deck.

METHOD: Stack the top twenty-six cards, making every second card a club in order from the ace to the king. In other words, the top card is an indifferent card, the next is the ace of clubs, the next is an indifferent card, the next is the deuce of clubs, etc.

False shuffle. Drop the deck on the table, instructing a spectator to deal until he feels like stopping. If he looks as if he may run past twenty-six cards (which seldom will be the case), tell him politely that you mean for him to stop sometime tonight—or something else to speed him up.

Secretly count as he deals. This is a bit harder to do than you would think, because you are apt to be talking. If he deals an even number, have him note the last card he dealt. If an odd number, have him look at the card that is now on top of the deck. In this way, you make sure he gets a club. What is more, you have only to divide the number at which his card lies by two—the result will be its numerical value. The rest is all a matter of showmanship.

Super Memory

EFFECT: The magician, after shuffling, takes a ridiculously quick glance at the faces of the cards and announces that he has memorized the top ten. He demonstrates by turning these ten cards, naming the value of each just before he turns it. He then repeats with the next ten cards.

METHOD: You simply stack twenty cards in an order you have previously memorized. Pick them up during the set-up location and put them on top. Casually false shuffle, glance at the faces of the cards and perform.

In order to memorize the values of two groups of ten cards without too much effort, you fall back on the old dodge of remembering sentences which suggest the order of the cards. For instance: "For (four) a (ace) sick (six) queen (queen) fifty- (five) five (five) jacks (jack) sang (seven)! to (two) God (king)." For the second ten cards, remember this one: "Ninety- (nine) nine (nine) kings (king) intended (ten) to (two) save (seven) jack (jack) for (four) a (ace) fortnight (four)."

The next trick doesn't require stacked cards and doesn't have to follow the set-up location. It fits into this chapter, however, because you prepare the deck for it right under the noses of the audience. It is a location performed under strict conditions and dressed up as a memory trick. I've fooled people with it who know a lot about cards.

The Photographic Eye

EFFECT: A spectator shuffles and cuts a deck which the magician need never have seen before. The magician gives the faces of the cards a lightning glance. He says that, while it is obviously impossible to memorize a deck in so short a time, one glance is enough to give him a lasting *impression* of the peculiarities of the sequence the cards happen to be in. Or something like that. If even one card were moved, he says, he would know it.

He spreads the deck on the table and turns his back. He instructs a spectator to slide a card out of the spread, peek at it, and return it to a place half a dozen cards or so away from its original position. The spectator squares the deck. The magician turns around, looks at the faces of the cards, and immediately announces the card which was moved!

Try to figure this one out before you read the secret.

METHOD: After the spectator has shuffled, take the cards from him. Square them. Hold them in your left hand with one end of the pack pointed toward you. Riffle this end, pretending to glance at the faces of the cards. Riffle with the right thumb-*nail,* cutting a *diagonal* scar across the end of the deck.

This scar is made up of a series of nicks, one in each of the fifty-two cards. It should run from the center of the bottom card diagonally toward a corner of the top card. It should be about twice the thickness of the pack in length. The action of riffling the cards covers the subterfuge perfectly.

The trick works itself from here on. Spread the cards quickly. Spread them in a straight line on the table, scarred end toward you. Turn your back and give the spectator his instructions. Let him square the deck and hand it to you. The nick on the end of the card that was moved will be plainly visible either above or below the diagonal scar, even if this card's position was changed by as few as six cards. Break the deck at this misplaced card. Note it as you glance at the faces of all the cards, and announce its name.

The scar should be clean and deep, rather than a vague, shallow scratch. Another way to scar a pack is to whack it on the table edge as you square up. Make this seem a casual action by hitting the deck once or twice more, but squarely on the table. If you use this latter method, scar the edge of the deck, not the end.

Chapter 11

Flourishes

*"Many things difficult to design
prove easy to performance."*

SAMUEL JOHNSON

This chapter briefly describes some fancy things to do with the pack—*flourishes*. They are feats of juggling, not mysteries. Yet they fit nicely into a program of tricks. They are good entertainment when done briskly and neatly —but they must be done very neatly indeed. A sloppy flourish, instead of making you look handy with the tickets, will inspire the thought that you ought to go home and brush up a mite.

Flourishes, especially fans, are most successful with a new deck that has been handled just enough to take the first stiffness out of it. A pack which has been used in a card game is usually hopeless. Cards treated so outlandishly lose their slickness from contact with the table top, and you might as well try to fan a bundle of old newspapers.

You will find some makes of cards more satisfactory for use in flourishes than others. You will also find that, for some obscure reason, there is definite variation in the fanning quality of different decks of the same brand and finish. Bicycle, Congress, Bee, and Aviator cards are generally satisfactory—brands that are universally obtainable.

Performers who go in for fans in a big way keep special decks for just this purpose. They separate the red and black cards for a contrasting display of colors, and they use colorful back designs. Dr. John Lewis, of Lasalle, Illinois, who presents as entertaining a routine of card fans as I've seen, has a deck made up of two decks with sharply contrasting backs. The number of different patterns Doc can twist that collection of cardboard into is truly amazing.

Flourishes are hard to put on paper because they depend on more than positions of cards and fingers. In different degrees, they require a springing of the cards that can be correctly determined only through trial and error. Perfecting a flourish is a question of nicety of pressure, so to speak. You'll know at once when you have hit on the knack. A couple of rainy evenings at home should be all you need to learn the comparatively easy flourishes described here.

One more word, and I'll get down to describing them.

Flourishes may be routined, and you may devote several minutes of your program to them exclusively. They may also be performed incidentally as you shuffle for a trick. A suddenly interpolated cascade or spring is surprising and is sometimes good misdirection. And, as you will see, fans have special deceptive uses.

To Spring the Cards

Hold the deck in the right hand, thumb at bottom end, fingers at top end. The back of the right hand is up. Place the left hand a few inches below the pack to catch the cards.

Slowly increase the pressure of your thumb and fingers until the cards spring in machine-gun sequence into the left palm. They must, to fall evenly, all shoot off the same end of the deck—preferably the thumb end.

When you can spring the cards evenly, try this: Begin with the pack in the left hand. Lift it with the right thumb and fingers, beginning the springing action as soon as the cards are an inch off the left palm. Quickly separate the hands and bring them together again as the last card is sprung. You seem to stretch and compress the deck like an accordion.

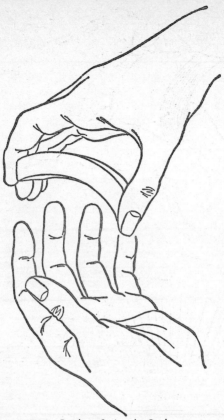

Ready to Spring the Cards

With a little practice, you can make the cards cover a distance of a foot or more.

The Cascade

Hold the deck as if you were going to spring it, but with its face to the left, edges parallel to the floor. Hold your left hand a few inches below the lower edge of the deck. Bow the deck. Bow it almost to the point where the cards spring. Now, very slowly, release the pressure to allow the cards to drop in an even ribbon into the left palm.

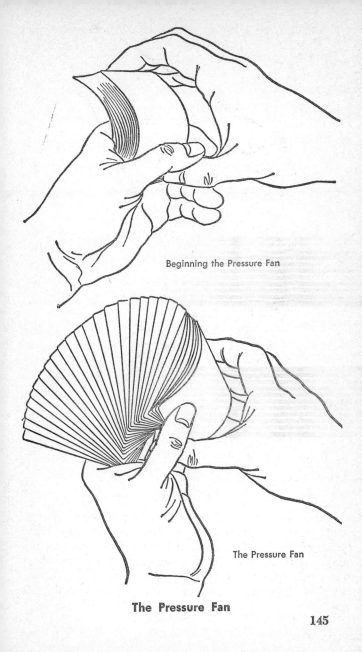

Beginning the Pressure Fan

The Pressure Fan

The Pressure Fan

Hold the cards at the tips of the right thumb and fingers as if you were going to spring them. Bend the ends forward, but not so hard as before. Put the left edge of the deck into the crotch of the left thumb. Three-quarters of the face of the bottom card should be exposed over the back of the left first finger.

The right fingers now twist the bent cards rapidly to the right, squeezing them into a perfectly even fan against the left finger tips. The cards should spread at least to the extent where they form a half-circle. When the fan is completed, the left thumb presses on the lower left corner of the top card to hold the cards in position.

To Close the Fan

To close the fan you have just made, neatly snapping it together with the left hand only, proceed as follows:

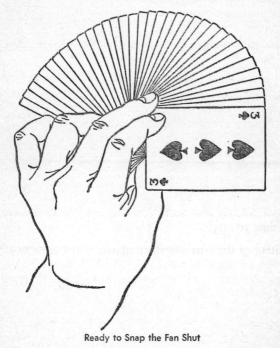

Ready to Snap the Fan Shut

Bend your left forefinger, placing its tip on the face of the bottom card of the deck (assuming that the faces of the cards are toward your palm) near the lower right corner of this card. Now bend the middle finger so that its tip touches the edge of this card at this same corner and also covers the edges of the next dozen cards. Extend the last two fingers so that they do not touch the cards—the fan is held only between the tips of the first and second fingers and the tip of the thumb.

Now bend the middle finger toward the palm, keeping its tip pressed against the cards. This will start the cards closing to the right, revolving between the first finger and thumb. Tilt the hand *slightly* to the right and then immediately to the left again. The motion to the right accelerates the closing action started by the middle finger, and the motion to the left is one of leveling the hand to catch the pack squarely at the conclusion of the flourish.

Eventually, you'll be able to dispense with the tilting of the hand.

The One-Hand Fan

Hold the deck by its end in the right hand. The thumb is on the back of the top card at the lower left corner. The fingers are on the bottom of the deck near the inner end. The tip of the third finger is directly opposite the thumb. The little finger barely touches the deck at the left edge—it plays no part in spreading the cards.

Press the thumb to the right and the fingers to the left. The fingers bend into the palm, holding the left part of the fan against the base of the thumb.

With a fairly new deck, you'll be able to do this fan the first time you try.

Either of the fans described above, when done neatly, is an impressive way to present the deck for the selection and return of a card. And they are not beyond adaptation to the ruses of the deceptionist.

For instance, make a two-hand fan and allow a spectator to choose a card from it. He will probably mess up your artistry a bit; so, as soon as he has the card, make another

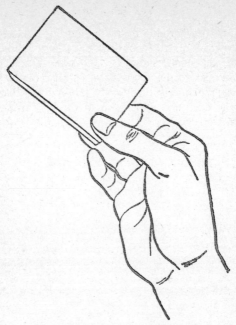

How to Hold Deck for the One-Hand Fan

fan and extend it for the return. Keep the cards pressed together so that his won't go quite all the way in.

Snap the fan shut with the left hand. You'll find the selected card neatly injogged, and you can easily get a break above it with the right thumb as you square the deck. Sometimes, cards above the selected one will protrude, too; but this makes no difference. If you have made sure that the spectator returned his card near the center, no card *below* it will be jogged; and it can still be easily cut to if there are a few sticking out above it.

The same principle may be applied to the one-hand fan. Pinch it as the card is returned, keeping this card from going all the way in. Immediately close the fan into the left hand, reversing the deck as you do so. Square the cards, getting your break at the injog.

148

The Blank Fan

A blank fan is made by spreading the cards to the left instead of to the right. Consequently, only a small section of blank pasteboard shows at each non-index corner, and the entire deck seems to consist of spotless cards. You may greatly heighten this illusion by having a blank card on top of the deck and slipping it to the bottom before you make the fan.

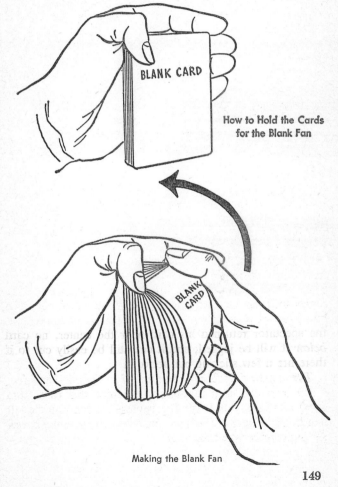

How to Hold the Cards
for the Blank Fan

Making the Blank Fan

An excellent way to make a blank fan is to hold the cards exactly as for the pressure fan, but with the positions of the right and left hands reversed. In other words, spread the cards with the left hand, making the fan in the right.

ANOTHER WAY: Hold the deck in the right hand as for the regular two-hand fan, but with the backs of the cards out. Turn the hand to the right so that the thumb end of the pack is up. Place the back of the pack against the left fingers with half of it projecting from the bottom of the left hand, squarely below the little finger. This finger is straight across the back of the top card at its center. Squeeze the cards, twisting them upward over the left fingers into a neat fan. Place the left thumb on the index corner of the bottom card and turn over the left hand to show the spotless faces of the cards.

Probably your first fan wasn't quite spotless. A little practice will teach you just how to spread the cards without revealing any ink. When you have the knack, try this:

Make the fan without spreading a packet at the face of the deck: fan only the first two-thirds of the cards. Turn over your fan to show it blank. Place the tip of the right middle finger against the left edge of the unspread packet. Press against this edge and draw your finger to the right, spreading the packet into a fan that suddenly reveals spots and that covers the blank fan.

The Rosette

The back of the deck is toward you, edges parallel to the floor. Place your right middle finger on the face of the bottom card parallel to and near the upper edge of the deck. The right end of the deck should be at the middle of the second joint of this finger. Place your left middle finger in a corresponding position at the diagonally opposite corner.

In other words, the index corners of the bottom card are exposed; each of the other corners is covered by a joint and a half of a middle finger. The thumbs are on the back of the deck, each opposite its own middle finger.

Here is one time you hold the deck tightly. Latch onto it

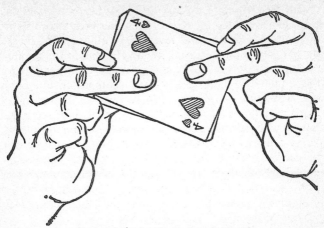

Beginning the Rosette (As Seen in Mirror)

as if it were a wad of horrid old hundred-dollar bills. Shove the middle fingers past each other, keeping them parallel. At the same time, make a circle with your thumbs, revolving the right one downward and the left upward. When you get the grip and action just right you'll be able to make a perfectly round rosette.

The Eye-Level Dovetail Shuffle

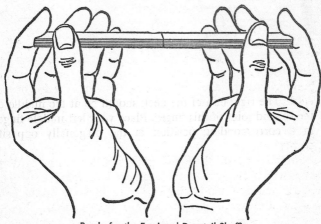

Ready for the Eye-Level Dovetail Shuffle

Cut the deck as equally as possible. Hold a half in each hand very much as a waiter holds a tray. Your fingers point toward the ceiling, and the packets are parallel to the floor, faces downward. A first finger is against one end of each packet. The thumb is on the inner edge, near this end. The last three fingers are on the opposite edge with the second finger directly across from the thumb.

Be sure the packets are well squared. Hold them at eye level and press their free ends together to make the cards bend downward. By releasing the pressure ever so slightly and moving one packet a thirty-second of an inch sideways, you can make the ends spring upward and neatly together.

You may find it easier to do this shuffle at the inner corners only, instead of along the whole length on the ends.

The interlacing action of the cards should occur in a flash. And the cards should alternate faultlessly when the shuffle is completed.

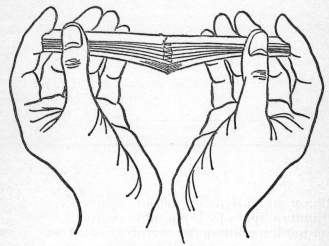

Springing the Cards Together

The Giant Fan of Cards

Do the eye-level shuffle. Push the interlaced packets one inch into each other. Take the deck where it is joined, holding it between the left thumb and fingers, and place the free end of one packet in the crotch of the right thumb. Hold the cards upright. You will find that the cards in the upper packet will be held firmly in position by the ends of the cards in the lower packet. (You may have to adjust the positions of the top and bottom cards to make sure that they are both in the lower packet.)

Place the left thumb against the left edges of the cards at the place where they are interlaced. The left fingers go be-

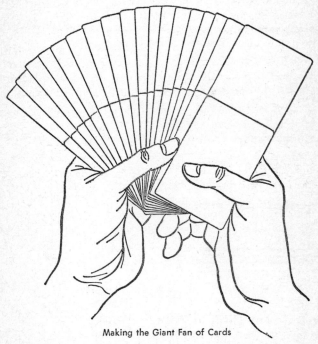

Making the Giant Fan of Cards

hind the cards. The top joint of the left middle finger presses against the right edges of the cards across from the thumb. The middle finger drags the cards to the left while the thumb spreads them in a series of rapid wiggling motions.

I know of no way to spring or squeeze this big fan into existence.

Chapter 12

More Impromptu Tricks

"Enough is equal to a feast."

HENRY FIELDING

PERHAPS BY this time you have taken to wearing an Inverness cape and a waxed mustache and have ordered some posters printed. Or perhaps you are fed up with this whole business of card trickery and have decided to take up the zither.

Probably you're between the two extremes. You've mastered a few good tricks but you're not quite ready to become a comic-strip character along with Mandrake the Magician and Harry Blackstone. You still feel as if you are wearing gloves when you try to deal bottoms and as if you have a loaf of bread, thin-sliced, in your hands when you practice the pass.

Don't worry because there are things in this book you can't do. There are plenty of long winter evenings ahead. Anyway, the important thing is whether you can mystify your friends—not whether you can balance the deck on a fingernail.

I'll tell you a secret. There are successful professional magicians who can't palm a postage stamp, sticky side in!

To complete your education, here are a few easy, mystifying tricks that originally were scattered among the various chapters but were cut for one reason or another. They are all impromptu tricks.

Change About

EFFECT: While the performer is out of the room, two spectators decide on a number between one and ten. One of them shuffles—let's suppose his name is Jimmy—and then notes the card that lies at the selected number from the top. The other spectator—Frances—notes the card that lies at the selected number from the bottom.

The magician returns. He briefly shuffles the cards. Jimmy counts down the selected number from the top again and removes the card that now lies there, leaving it face down on the table. Frances counts up from the bottom of the deck, just as she did before, and places the card that now lies there on the table beside Jimmy's. She keeps her finger on it.

Jimmy and Frances name their original selections. When the cards on the table are turned over, Frances has Jimmy's card and he has hers!

METHOD: It's all in the shuffle. You reverse the order of the top ten cards and put them on the bottom; then you reverse the order of the bottom ten cards and put them on top.

Shuffle overhand, as follows: Run ten cards off the top into your left hand. Shuffle haphazardly until you have a few more than ten cards in your right hand. Shuffle these last cards singly onto the top of the deck. Give the deck a false cut and drop it on the table.

Shuffle rapidly, but above all smoothly. Don't give the impression that the shuffle is for any purpose but to destroy the order of the deck. Emphasize the point that you couldn't possibly know what number Jimmy and Frances selected.

The Count-Down Trick

About the first trick I learned, back when I had to look twice to tell the difference between a king and a jack, was the old chestnut where a selected card appears at a number named by the spectator. It has held up through heaven-knows-how-many generations and it is still good. Recalling the different versions of this trick that I've done, it occurs to me that these variations of a principle offer an instructive example of the evolution of a trick.

The first way I learned the trick was, after getting the selected card to the top, to count down to whatever number the spectator named and turn the wrong card. I reversed the cards as I counted, bringing the selected card to the right position when they were replaced on the deck. So, I would say, "I missed it. Maybe we'll have better luck if you try it." And, of course, we did.

(I claim to be the only trickster who ever fooled himself with this trick. I did it on a train once with a dog-eared deck that I happened to pick up. The spectator, a traveling salesman, selected a card and named a number. I got his card to the top, counted off the number, and turned the last card. It was the right one. I'd hit it the first time! The salesman was only mildly surprised, but I was one astonished lad. The answer? It was a pinochle deck.)

Later, when I had learned the gambler's shuffle, I nonchalantly shuffled after the spectator named his number. I ran his number of cards, injogged, and cut. His card would then turn up in the right place on the first count.

Next, Dr. John Lewis showed me a simple and effective way to do the trick. When you have got the card to the top, you count to the spectator's number by reversing the cards rapidly into the right hand. When you reach the number, you slap the packet of reversed cards face up onto the top of the deck, exposing the chosen card. This creates the illusion that you fairly reveal the card at the selected number.

Finally, I developed the following method:

Get the card to the top. Have a number named—let's suppose it is six. Hold the deck in the left hand in position for dealing. Shove the top card to the right with the left thumb. Take it with the right hand with the first three fingers on its face and thumb on its back. The little finger is bent in toward the palm. Count, "One." Shove the next card under the right thumb on top of the first; but just before you do so, straighten the right little finger so that it is between the two cards near their inner ends. Count, "Two."

Shove the next three cards, one at a time, directly above the second card. Count, "Three, four, five."

Place the packet of cards in your right hand directly on top of the deck, as if you were taking the sixth card *under* the first five. The left thumb moves out of the way to the upper left corner of the deck. Count, "Six," and at the same time shove the bottom card of the right-hand packet (the selected card) to the left with the right fingers. Turn it face

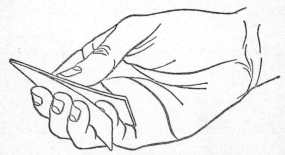

The Count-Down Trick—Showing How Break is Held

up with the right fingers and left thumb as if it were the sixth card. Shove this face-up card onto the ones in the right hand and display it there. If the counting is done rhythmically, the illusion is perfect.

The Salt Trick

EFFECT: A spectator shuffles. He cuts the pack into three packets, notes a card on top of any of these packets, and assembles the deck. The magician throws the deck onto the table so that the cards spread. Quick as a flash, he picks out the selected card and turns it up.

METHOD: Carry a little salt in your vest pocket. When the spectator is peeking at his card, dip into this pocket and get a few grains on the tips of your fingers. Point to one of the packets and say, "Put that packet on top of this one." Touch the top of "this one," which is the packet with the selected card. Brush your thumb against your finger tips to leave a few grains of salt on this card.

When the deck is assembled, hold it a few inches above

the table and throw it forward end first. The bottom card hits the table flatly and the rest of the cards coast forward in a line. The deck will break slightly where you have inserted the salt, which acts as ball bearings. The card below this break will be the selected one.

Sand works as well as salt.

The Magnetic Cards

EFFECT: The performer shows two cards that are together in the pack. He separates them by several cards. When the deck is spread face up, these two cards are found together again.

METHOD: Cut the deck, leaving one of the halves on the table. Lift the top two cards of the half in your hands, showing them as one card. Call attention to its identity. Then show the next card. Return these two (really three) cards to the top of the packet; then lift off the top card and, without showing its face place it on top of the packet on the table. The spectators think it is the first card of the two you have just shown. Cut the packet on the table, carry the cut, and place the assembled packet on the one in your hand. Apparently, you have separated the two cards. Spread the pack face up and show that they are together again.

The Windmill

Suppose you have, in the language of the card-man, *controlled* a selected card to a position second from the top. Snap the deck and announce that you have made it jump to the top. Push the top card to the right with your left thumb. Take its upper right corner between the thumb and finger of the right hand with the thumb on the face of the card. Show this card by turning it end over end.

Rest your right little finger tip against the upper right corner of the deck. Shove the top card (the selected one) a bit to the right and clip its corner between the tips of the right third and middle fingers.

The spectator says that the card you are showing him is

not his. You seem surprised and say that that's too bad—you wanted to bring the trick to a sudden climax. Return the exposed card to the deck by reversing the end-over-end action, but retain your grip on the next card. It will reveal itself so suddenly that no one will see exactly where it comes from. This is a flourish, I suppose, rather than a deep, dark mystery; but it is an amusing way to produce a selected card. I am told that it should be credited to that master card manipulator, Paul LePaul.

The Court Card Location

EFFECT: The twelve court cards are picked out of the deck and placed on top. A spectator counts down any number less than twelve and notes the card at that number. He replaces the counted-off cards. He now gives the deck a dovetail shuffle. And another dovetail shuffle. Another spectator cuts.

You find the card.

METHOD: The court cards may be in any order but you must know the top card. Make sure that the spectator reverses the cards as he counts. When he replaces them, the card you know will be just above the selected one. The dovetail shuffles and the cut don't mean a thing! They may separate your key card from the chosen one, but *no court cards* will be between the two. The first court card below your key card will be the selected one.

Magic by Long Distance

EFFECT: The magician telephones a friend who has lots of time and who is just crazy about card tricks. The friend provides himself with a pack of cards. The magician asks him to take a number between one and ten. The friend says, for instance, six.

The magician says, "Deal six cards into a packet on the table. . . . Look at the top card of the packet. Write its name on your telephone pad. Now, think of another number. Don't tell me this one. Deal that many cards onto the packet already on the table. . . . Done that? Look at the card that is now on top of the packet on the table. Remember this card. Take a moment to fix it in your mind. Put it on top of the deck and put the packet of cards on top of it. Now, read me the top twenty cards of the deck in order."

The friend does so.

The magician says, "Now, shuffle. . . . You have chosen two cards. One you are remembering. The name of the other is written on your telephone pad. Tell me the name of either of these, and tell me which it is."

"The eight of clubs," the friends says, "is written on the pad."

"The queen of diamonds," the magician says, "is the other."

Which is correct.

METHOD: Unknown to your victim, you jot down the twenty top cards as he read them to you. Your list will look something like this:

9D, 4D, KH, 4C, KD, JS, 7H, 8C, 2S, KS, 5C, 5S, 2D, QD, 9H, 3C, QH, JD, 9S, 10C.

You know the first number counted. Because the counted-off cards were placed on top of his second selection, that card will lie at that number below his first selection. In the example given, the first number was six. Therefore, the queen of diamonds (his second card) is the sixth card below the eight of clubs (his first card).

If he tells you the name of the first card, count six cards to the right. If he tells you the name of the second, count six to the left.